God's Funeral

Psychology:
Trading the Sacred for the Secular

David M. Tyler

God's Funeral
Psychology:
Trading the Sacred for the Secular

©2009 by David M. Tyler

Published by FOCUS PUBLISHING
All Rights Reserved

Scripture references are quoted from
The New American Standard Version of the Bible
Where noted, the King James Version
and the New King James Version

Cover design by Melanie Schmidt

Printed in the United States of America

Focus Publishing
Post Office Box 665
Bemidji, MN   56619
All Rights Reserved

Dedication

To my wife
Pam

Table of Contents

Introduction
The Triumph of the Therapeutic

The triumph of the therapeutic can perhaps best be understood as the ascendancy of a substitute faith... psychoanalysis has assumed many of the functions traditionally performed by religion, and has done so by translating many of the theological and existential issues of human life into therapeutic terms.

Charles J. Sykes,
A Nation of Victims

To seek out therapy today is to stick your hand into a grab bag of theories that often utterly contradict each other in their specific assumptions but that agree on a more general unproved assertion that the therapist has the knowledge and techniques allowing him or her to see into the most fundamental and hidden motivations of the mind.

Ethan Watters and **Richard Ofshe,**
Therapy's Delusions

Our culture is in trouble today. The weakness of the evangelical church, which has been disemboweled of its theological character, is all the more troubling. The shaping of the church's mind, generally speaking, has been left to the psychologists. Its taste for anything psychology-related appears to be insatiable and has led the church, with disastrous consequences, down the road of accommodation and compromise. Today's theology is a hybrid, a blend of two antithetical worldviews, in which what is popular and psychological eclipses what is sound theologically. Rooted in atheistic Darwinism, the biblical model replaced by the therapeutic leaves no space for man made in the image and likeness of his Creator. We have surrendered to psychology's biological fate and describe ourselves in terms of genes, self-image, gender, sexual orientation and a host of disorders. The theological concepts of sin, guilt and responsibility have lost their relevance. To say we have disemboweled or eviscerated evangelicalism's theological character is to say it has been gutted of its biblical substance and meaning. We have traded sacred for secular. Instead of spiritual beings set apart for a sacred purpose, we are seen as material beings, and life is a series of problems to be solved by professionals. Today, when faced with problems we seek a therapist. In the past, when faced with the same problems, we would seek God. Now we think secularly about the most sacred things.

The Apostle Paul wrote, **"For the wrath of God is revealed from heaven against all *ungodliness* and *unrighteousness* of men who suppress the truth in unrighteousness"** (Romans 1:18, emphasis mine). Simply stated, we cannot have righteousness without godliness. It is a fallacy that we can shed ourselves of God and at the same time we hold on to righteousness and morality. The order is important. Paul puts ungodliness first and unrighteousness second. Ungodliness flows naturally into unrighteousness. An ungodly people will be an unrighteous people. Once you have godliness, righteousness and morality follow. Today we are trying to have righteousness without godliness and the facts demonstrate it cannot be done.

"'Ungodliness' refers to perversity that is religious in character, 'unrighteousness' to what is moral; the former is illustrated by idolatry, the latter by immorality."[1] 'Ungodliness'

[1] John Murray, *The New International Commentary on the New Testament, The Epistle to the Romans*, (Grand Rapids, MI, William B. Eerdmans Publishing Co., 1959), p. 36.

Romans 1:18-32

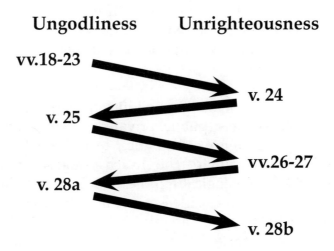

Ungodliness	Unrighteousness
vv.18-23	
	v. 24
v. 25	
	vv.26-27
v. 28a	
	v. 28b

(asebeia) focuses on man's attitude toward God. It means simply to live as though God does not exist. It means disregard or defiance toward "God's Person." On the other hand, 'unrighteousness' (adikia) focuses on man's attitude or actions towards others. It is wrong doing. Paul maintains this distinction through the rest of the chapter.

The consequence of ungodliness is unrighteousness, but the consequence of unrighteousness is bad feelings. Behavior affects the way a person feels. It is a principle found first in Genesis 3, and throughout the entire Bible. Ungodliness leads to unrighteousness which leads to guilt, depression, anxiety, fear, shame, and so on. Bad behavior triggers unpleasant feelings as a way to warn us that we have violated God's standard. Emotional "pain" should be viewed as a symptom in the same way abdominal pain that warns a person of an infected appendix.

In order to deal with these uncomfortable feelings and the problems that accompany them society takes on a psychological mindset. God is pronounced dead or at best banished into some far-off secluded place in the universe. Unfettered by divine influence, man concocts literally hundreds of "healing" theories and therapies. With therapeutic warmth and acceptance, value-free diagnoses are made of people's wounds and hurts. Sin is domesticated in order to support these secular notions about man and his problems.

Psychology has spread like wildfire throughout America. We find it in the schools (public, private, Christian and home), workplace, legal system, and politics, to name a few. What about the Christian Church? The church would seem to be one area where the psychological mindset would be absent. After all, Christianity promotes ideas such as self-sacrifice, moral absolutes and truth, which are antithetical to a psychological worldview. Nevertheless, Christianity now incorporates at least some elements of psychological ideology. God is assigned psychiatric capabilities, and is more like a counselor who responds to individual needs and feelings than a judge who condemns sinners and blesses the faithful. This is clearly evident among American evangelicals (some of the most conservative Protestants), who have embraced a psychological worldview.

Psychology, which promises people the good life and how to live it, has replaced traditional beliefs. Those who once took comfort from the words of God and worshipped at the altar of Yahweh, now take solace and worship at the altars of Freud, Jung, Rogers, and a host of others. The words of Jesus Christ was once the common focal point, but today it is the theories, therapies and psycho-language of Dr. Feelgood who promises personal change, peace of mind, development of potentials and more satisfying sex.

The triumph of the therapeutic, as sociologist Phillip Rieff refers to it in his book of the same title, has several characteristics or doctrines:

1. __It promotes the concept that life and the world around us are best understood and interpreted in psychological terms__. Other explanations of life and the world as found in the Old and New Testaments are supplanted by the therapeutic mindset. We commonly think psychologically, not biblically, of ourselves and others. We think in terms of depression, anxiety, insecurity, self-esteem, inhibitions, obsessions, unconscious desires, emotional pain, trauma, hurts and so on. The deeds of the flesh described by the Apostle Paul in Galatians 5:19-20 are no longer considered to be sins, but psychological diseases. A person only has to browse the bookshelves of a Christian bookstore to see how widely accepted are the works and thoughts of Sigmund Freud, Carl Rogers, Abraham Maslow and other secular counselors.

2. __It promotes the idea that observable behavior is only the tip of the iceberg__. In the ocean, only a small portion of an iceberg is visible. The bulk of an iceberg is out of sight below the surface of the water. There is so much, we are told, we do not know about ourselves. Words and actions have hidden meaning. What looks like confidence is really a person compensating for a lack of confidence. What appears to be pride is a person compensating for low self-esteem. Nothing is what it seems. There is no certainty. There are innumerable possibilities and interpretations. What appears to be is in fact the opposite. What seems to be trivial is full of significance. What looks significant is trivial. Introspection is the main activity. We wonder what our actions and feelings mean. We look for signs and clues. We pay a therapist to help us unravel all the possibilities and understand the contradictions. All this reinforces the psychological mindset.

3. __It promotes the idea that we are not as happy, healthy and productive as we should be__. The psychological mindset would liberate us from traditionalism and all its hassles, restrictions and abuse. Freud saw religion and Christianity in particular, as restrictive and part of the problem. Carl Rogers praised the psychological mindset for its freedom from fixed beliefs such as Christianity. The focus of therapy is to liberate and expand the

self. We suffer from a variety of inadequacies and deficits. We feel we are not okay. Our life is not working. We are basically good and have unlimited potential. The problem is our individual self has been subdued by repressive and oppressive people, traditions and institutions such as the family, church, society, etc. These have produced guilt, frustration, anxiety, depression and therefore, we must break free in order to grow.

4. <u>The psychological mindset promotes the idea that everyone can benefit</u> from therapy. In light of the fact that we all have problems and are not as creative, happy and healthy as we should be, it follows logically that we all could benefit from therapy. Even therapists themselves are huge consumers of therapy. The idea that people are incapable of dealing with difficulties, traumas and problems in their lives is entrenched in the psychological mindset. Dealing with the loss of a loved one these days, we are told, takes the expertise of a therapist. Years ago people survived their grief quite well by themselves and perhaps the comfort they gleaned from family, friends and pastor.

5. <u>The expert therapist knows what is best for us</u>. The goal of therapy is the individual's freedom. The paradox, however, is that in practice therapeutic freedom is freedom from everything and everyone else except the therapist. The therapist's guidance is vital to living our life successfully and realizing our full potential. The therapist can see into the heart and correctly evaluate and diagnose the problem. He knows what is right for us. We accept the idea that the counselor knows more than we know. We willingly turn to them and follow their advice even when it may sound strange and contrary to what we think and are inclined to do.

The warm and cordial acceptance of psychology found fertile ground in America's belief that one could overcome every obstacle and achieve whatever one set out to do. It is the belief that we can dream dreams and master our own destiny no matter what. It is the attitude of autonomy, self-reliance and self-fulfillment.

Psychology offers us the power to be whole, assertive, and achieve self-understanding which will help us realize our full potential. Much of this optimism and confidence has been fueled by advancements in technology. Technology has given us a plethora of gadgets and machines that have made our lives comfortable and entertaining. Technology makes our jobs and chores easier and we finish sooner. We have more time to play. In part, it was our growing dependence upon technology that contributed to the shift toward the "expert" mentality. We need an expert or specialist to fix our cars, homes, and our bodies. Years ago, when life was simpler, people were more self-reliant. They could fix their own cars, but today's automobiles are equipped with computers and high-tech satellite positioning devices. We cannot understand everything, so experts are essential. Why shouldn't we expect them to help us reach our full potential and guide us in solving our relationship difficulties? Soon "experts" on life and living displaced the pastor, priest and rabbi.

The therapeutic and evangelical practices began merging in the 1960s and continue to this day. The pervasiveness of the psychological mindset, with its most notable symbol being Sigmund Freud, a cigar smoking atheist preoccupied by drugs and sex, demonstrates how evangelicalism has succumbed to a secular drift unmatched in Christian history. The Christian view of man and his problems has been significantly diminished within the church. There is still a Christian ethic, practice, and spirituality. Christians, as church members, assume their obligations and observe the ordinances ignored by unbelievers. As spiritual men and women, they endeavor to cultivate their relationship with God through Scripture and prayer unknown and undesired by unbelievers. However, like unbelievers, when it comes to the nature of man, his behaviors, feelings and moods, the modern Christian has succumbed to secularization. The church, except for those in the Nouthetic Counseling movement, has accepted a frame of reference constructed by secularists, most of whom were and are atheists. Tragically, denominational publishing houses Christianize these anti-Christian theories in their magazines, teaching materials and books. With all the fervor evangelicals are known for, they promote psychology.

Chapter One
God's Funeral: "Ungodliness"

For the wrath of God is revealed from heaven against all *ungodliness* and unrighteousness of men who suppress the truth in unrighteousness.
Apostle Paul, Romans 1:18
(Italics mine)

Thomas Hardy, an English poet and atheist, wrote a poem in which he imagined himself attending God's funeral. The coffin carried "a strange and mystic form" to its, or His, final resting place. Stanza thirteen says,

> Some in the background then I saw,
> Sweet women, youths, men, all incredulous,
> Who chimed: 'This is a counterfeit of straw,
> This requiem mockery! Still he lives to us!'

Hardy saw the cold stare of disbelief on the faces of the mourners. They were unwilling to admit or accept God as dead. God is not dead, "this is a counterfeit of straw," they lamented. Their words, "Still he lives to us," drew the sympathy of Hardy, for these courageous believers who continued to worship a dead God.

A Divided World

"The fool has said in his heart, 'There is no God'" (Psalm 14:1). A culture dominated by the *ideas* of fools will soon lead to a culture where foolishness and ungodliness look like wisdom. This could not be truer than in our present day.

We live in a divided world. I am not referring to geographical boundaries and borders. Look at the religious and cultural beliefs deeply held by people which constitute their worldviews. James Sire, in his book, *The Universe Next Door*, defines a worldview as "a set of presuppositions (assumptions which may be true, partially true or entirely false) which we hold (consciously or subconsciously, consistently or inconsistently) about the basic makeup of our world."[2]

A person's worldview functions in much the same way as colored eyeglasses. Everything will look green to a person wearing green-colored glasses. The same objects will look red to a person wearing red-tinted eyeglasses. This explains why people with different worldviews often see the same facts in a different way. One person looks at a butterfly and is moved by the splendor of God who created it. Another looks at the same butterfly and is moved by evolution's ability to make such a delicate insect. In counseling, one counselor looks at a person's behavior and sees a sickness that is said to be caused by a chemical imbalance in the brain that could be corrected through the use of medications. The other counselor looks at the same person and sees rebellion and sin. In the latter example it is not the facts (the person's behavior), but the interpretation of those facts (sin vs. sickness) which determines the diagnosis.

The presence of many alternative worldviews is the defining characteristic of contemporary culture. We live in a multicultural, pluralistic age. The range of perspectives stands in sharp contrast to the traditional Judeo-Christian Western viewpoint that affirmed God as Creator of moral truth. The Renaissance and Enlightenment periods changed everything. Human beings now claim divine prerogative to conceptualize reality and shape and define man's nature as he pleases. This has had tremendous

2 James W. Sire, *The Universe Next Door*, (Downers Grove, IL: InterVarsity Press, 1997), p. 16.

influence in virtually every field, every discipline of study, every level of education and practice, including counseling.

Ideas have consequences just like causes have effects. However, there is a deeper reality to consider when reflecting upon the worldview discord of our time. A clash of worldviews, from a Christian perspective, also assumes a hidden, unseen dimension. To Christians there is a spiritual battle between the kingdom of God and the kingdom of Satan in which truth itself is at stake. The prize is how men understand God, themselves, the universe and their place in it. Therefore, it is not surprising that a worldview war is at the center of the conflict between God and Satan.

The theistic worldview, which is the belief in a triune personal God who created the universe, made man in His image and likeness, revealed Himself, and could be known, clearly dominated the Western world up to the end of the seventeenth century. Christians did not always agree on everything. There were, as there are now, squabbles among believers, but those disagreements were argued and the lines were drawn within the circle of theism.

Christianity had so penetrated the Western world that from the Middle Ages to the seventeenth century very few challenged the existence of God or held that ultimate reality was impersonal and the death of an individual meant extinction. Even people who rejected Jesus Christ as their Lord and Savior lived in fear of being held accountable for the sins committed in this life. They knew they were bad by Christian standards.

With the proliferation of worldviews this, of course, is no longer true. The next person you meet could adhere to any one of a dozen distinctly different views of understanding what life is all about.

An Easy Revolution

The rallying cry of revolutionaries is always injustice whether it is racial, economic or social. Revolutions are usually turbulent times of rapid and broad changes. Old ways, conventions, structures, beliefs and values are swept away. The overthrow of one government or ruler is substituted for another. Those who enjoyed the lion's share of wealth, pleasure and power are stripped of their privileges and exiled in one form or another. The revolutionaries now bask in their supremacy. This is the way revolutions typically happen.

Today in America there is a revolution of a different kind. The fact that our Western culture is being upended is no surprise; the interesting thing about it is the relative ease by which this revolution has occurred. It has not been brutal or vicious, but innocuous and nearly inconspicuous. The guerrillas are ordinary people who would be appalled if they could see themselves at the center of this secular reformation. They are not your typical wild-eyed, rabble-rousing revolutionaries. They are both unbelievers and believers. They are not provocative. They are mild-mannered revolutionaries who have affected every nook and cranny of Western society. The change they have wrought has not been merely in the outer fabric of our culture in technology, economics and politics. This change has been in the deepest sense, *spiritual*. It has made inroads into that place deep inside all of us where values are shaped and meaning is constructed. It has assaulted our inner lives and swept those values and beliefs overboard. Our society has changed. We have changed. The church has changed. Why are we not angry?

God is Dead – Ungodliness

The pre-modern phase of Western society believed in God. Most people, whether they were Christian or not, believed basic Christian concepts. They believed in the spiritual realm beyond the senses. This does not mean, however, that Western culture was characterized by a monolithic worldview (one worldview). The beliefs included mythological paganism, classical rationalism, as well as biblical revelation.

The classical Greek thinkers, Socrates, Plato and Aristotle, contributed a great deal to the amount of knowledge in our Western culture. They are recognized for laying much of the foundation of our heritage with their emphasis on the rational order of the universe as proof of the existence of a higher being. Socrates believed the universe was under the control of a single Divine Spirit. In teaching his views, Socrates challenged the polytheistic beliefs of the day. Ultimately, Socrates was sentenced to death because he rejected the mythological gods (worldview), arguing there must be only one supreme God.

Plato, a student of Socrates, also viewed the world as being the work of a single and transcendent God. He argued that the order and arrangement of the world must be due to the work of a Soul or Mind. He opposed the Greek philosopher-scientists who believed and tried to account for the order in nature by means of mechanical principles. Aristotle, a student of Plato, believed in the immortality of the soul. When he looked at the orderliness of the creation, Aristotle surmised that it came about not by chance but by the hand of a craftsman, which was God.

The Greeks fashioned a different way of looking at their world. Their belief in a transcendent God, however vague, was a major step in the right direction. However, they were still pagan and their doctrines were incompatible with biblical truth. By the time Paul and the other Apostles made their missionary journeys, the Greek world was ready for the Gospel.

The Judeo-Christian part of our heritage was adopted from the old nation of Israel. The descendants of Abraham had an unwavering faith in one God. Whether they were in Israel or in exile, the entire structure of Jewish life was regulated daily by Mosaic rules and regulations intended as reminders of their past. They believed their laws had been given by God Himself to Moses, their patriarch, and were consequently a divine revelation. When Jesus of Nazareth came on the scene, He spoke about God from personal experience. He defied the laws of nature by performing miraculous deeds such as healing the sick and raising the dead. His claim to be the Son of God and his criticism of the Levitical priesthood's embellishment of the Mosaic Law threatened their livelihood. He was condemned to death. His subsequent death and resurrection proved to be the greatest stumbling block of all. The final blow to the orthodox Jewish mind came when it became known that the promise of eternal life was not the exclusive blessing of Israel, but was available to the Gentiles as well (Acts 22:21-22).

The biblical and classical worldviews did not always completely and in every detail fit together. There were obvious differences. However, Socrates, Plato, and Aristotle argued that there was a transcendent reality beyond this world which gave the world meaning. They believed the physical world was orderly and to some extent knowable. They agreed upon the objectivity of truth and absolutes. For these reasons many Christian thinkers, such as Thomas Aquinas (1225-1274), adopted portions of classical philosophy as intellectual tools to give expression to their biblical faith. Aquinas tried to reconcile the irreconcilable by placing revelation and human reason on an equal footing. The result was that Greek philosophy could only be harmonized with biblical theology at the expense of biblical theology. Aquinas's views opened the door to human reason, pushing revelation and God further into the background. Man was left to rely on his own intellect. Greek humanism had thus been introduced into Christian theology. Centuries later in 1879, Pope Leo XIII would declare the eternal validity of Aquinas's theology. His theological system would direct the beliefs and lifestyle of the world's Roman Catholics.

This mingling of biblical revelation, classical rationalism and pagan mythologies dominated Western civilization for hundreds of years. During the middle ages, under a thin covering of Christianity, pagan gods were given the names of Christian saints. The Gospel was obscured. Biblical truth was compromised by human reason and pagan superstition. The old Roman church was headed for a great schism.

It was not until the period of the Renaissance that the mingling of the classical rationalism and biblical revelation was reversed. Renaissance humanism rediscovered and reasserted the Greeks and the Reformation rediscovered and reasserted the Bible. It was a period marked by a humanistic revival of classical influence of art, literature and modern science. The Bible, translated into the language of common people, brought a spiritual revival. Martin Luther's view of *sola Scriptura* challenged the absolute authority of the church. Papal and ecclesiastical authority was replaced by Protestants with biblical authority.

Many of the early scientists, such as Isaac Newton, Johann Kepler and Louis Pasteur, were Christians who believed nature to be the good and orderly work of a personal God.[3] However, the discovery of the great laws of the universe gave credibility to the view that all reality conformed to those laws. For example, Isaac Newton discovered and published the laws of gravity. Newton's discovery encouraged the belief that the universe operated strictly by mathematical laws. The consequence of these findings was the determination that divine intervention was unnecessary, thus reducing the cosmos, all life, and man himself to mere mechanism.

---

3   Henry M. Morris has written extensively on this subject in his book *The Biblical Basis for Modern Science*, (Grand Rapids, MI: Baker Book House, 1984).

The Period of Enlightenment

The progress of science accelerated so rapidly that it seemed as if science could explain everything. God was unnecessary. It was reasoned that with a universe of laws, there was no place for divine intervention. God had set the universe in motion, and then disappeared, allowing natural laws alone to govern it. This is called Deism and is a stepping stone between a theistic worldview and an atheistic worldview.

The pre-modern ideas merged into what is called the Modern Age or the Age of Enlightenment. By the early 1700s, a drum began to sound for a complete liberation of reason from biblical revelation. Christian supernaturalism became outdated. People became disenchanted with teachings based on the Bible, that is, the teachings that had been combined with tradition by the Roman Catholic Church. This naturally led to the skepticism of the "free-thinkers," such as Voltaire and Rousseau, who saw religion as the root of man's problem. They turned from revelation to reason in their quest for truth.

The Enlightenment had enthroned science. Its thinkers embraced classicism, but without the supernaturalism of Plato and Aristotle, with its order and rationality. Christianity was put in the same category as paganism with its superstitions and considered "unenlightened." The creed was autonomy and the overthrow of all external authority. Thus the modern person began to take shape. Human reason became the source of morality and meaning. Previously, enlightened thinkers related moral absolutes to a higher being, but soon began to answer ethical questions in terms of a closed system. This new approach was called utilitarianism.

Utilitarianism decides moral issues by studying the effect of an action upon society as a whole and not by appealing to transcendent absolutes. A behavior is considered wrong if it has a negative effect and right if it has a positive effect on society. Stealing is wrong not because the Bible says it is wrong, but because stealing has a detrimental effect and interferes with the way an economy functions. The rule is if it makes the economy function more efficiently then it is good. It is wrong if it interferes with the operation of society. Without God, a pragmatic approach is the means whereby men face moral issues.

Enlightenment science, by removing God from human affairs, set the stage for secular humanism. Humanism requires the theory of evolution in order to maintain the idea that there never has been and never will be any divine intervention. In 1859, Charles Darwin published *The Origin of Species,* which provided an interpretive grid that was laid over the whole of life. It spilled over into the arts, architecture, philosophy, theology, history, science, and psychology. It was the intellectual track by which the pre-modern world moved into the modern.

Enlightenment thinking was believed to set man free to dream dreams of a utopian world with man standing proud at its center. It would be an ideal place where man would lean only on his own reason and goodness. The demand was freedom from the past, freedom from God, and freedom from authority. It unequivocally opposed all ideas grounded in what was eternal, fixed and unchanging. It was considered the next step in human development and maturity. A new way of knowing, exemplified best in science, would enable man to increasingly harness nature. In application, this new knowledge would produce an out-pouring of technology and the production of goods, raising the quality of life for everyone. Poverty would be eliminated. In authority, man would be able to make rational decisions pertaining to life without being held back by the pressures and perversions of "superstitions" from the past, i.e. religion. Man would become an autonomous being, "skeptical of orthodoxies, rebellious against authority…responsible for his own beliefs and actions…assured of his intellectual capacity to comprehend and control nature…and altogether less dependent on an omnipotent God."[4] Man himself became the source for morality and from which to draw explanations about life. He would construct his own meaning. And so it was with great optimism, with the passing of God, mankind stepped into the great era of enlightenment.

Romanticism

The consensus among modern and enlightened man was that he was now on the road to a perfect world. The danger was that without a heavenly or transcendent road map to guide him, serious arguments would arise on how to get there. One such revolt against rationalism's sterile, mechanistic way was a movement called Romanticism. Although love may occasionally be the subject of Romantic art, Romanticism had little to do with things normally thought to be "romantic." Rather, it was a philosophical movement that redefined the fundamental ways in which people in Western cultures thought about themselves and about their world. The thinkers of the Enlightenment emphasized the supremacy of deductive reasoning. Romanticism cultivated subjectivity and personal experience. It elevated intuition, imagination, emotionalism and feeling. Romanticism followed a biological model and explained nature in terms of a life force animating the entire universe including human beings. Enlightenment thinkers saw the universe as one giant lifeless machine. Romanticism encouraged people to get in touch with their feelings. By opening one's self up to nature one could "become one with nature" achieving unity with the life force. This life force, like Deism, served as the basis of a new secular religion pushing God further to the outside. The squabble between the Rationalists and Romantics continued through most of the nineteenth century.

---

4 Richard Tarnas, *The Passion of the Western Mind: Understanding the Ideas That Have Shaped Our World View*, (New York, NY: Harmony Books, 1991), p. 282.

Darwin's theory of evolution challenged Romanticism just as it challenged Christianity. Unlike the idealistic romantics who saw nature as being good, Darwin described nature as being intrinsically violent. The "survival of the fittest" was the fundamental law. The strong preyed upon the weak. Romanticism succumbed to neo-Enlightenment materialism in the latter half of the nineteenth century. A new worldview, existentialism, emerged from the bleak facts of materialism.

Existentialism

Existentialism teaches that there is no meaning or purpose to life. Life is absurd. It makes no sense. The blind and automatic repetitions of natural laws are inhuman and meaningless. The individual creates his own meaning by the choices he makes in life. Choice becomes the ultimate value. Choice is elevated to the only justification for any action a person may take. For example, "pro-choice" advocates are not concerned about the morality of abortion. They are not interested in objective information concerning fetal development. They are not concerned with how abortions are performed. They are disinterested in the philosophical arguments about human life. Arguments from the outside world are meaningless and have no bearing on a woman's private choice to get an abortion.

The existentialist, having decided that there is no transcendent purpose, no redemption, no answer to life's dilemmas, is free falling in a vacuum of pessimism and despair. Life is a temporary diversion. All his dreams and projects have no significance. Existentialist philosopher Albert Camus said if God truly is dead, then "there is [only] one truly serious philosophical problem, and that is suicide. Judging whether life is or is not worth living amounts to answering the fundamental question of philosophy."[5]

---

5 Albert Camus, "Absurd Reasoning," *The Myth of Sisyphus*, trans. Justin O'Brien (New York, NY: Alfred A. Knopf, 1969), p. 3.

The movie, *They Shoot Horses, Don't They?* is a 1969 film that portrays several contestants in a Depression-era dance marathon. The participants struggling to survive the hard times continue to dance in the hope of winning a cash prize. From time to time the master of ceremonies would require the music to be played in double-time, quickening the pace in order to wear down the couples and force more of them to drop out of the contest. "Round and round and round they go," he would recite into the microphone, "where they stop, nobody knows." The quickening tempo was a grueling experience for already wearied dancers. One contestant suffered a heart attack. The movie graphically portrays the existentialist's dark and impassionate outlook on life.

The same theme is featured in the Old Testament book of Ecclesiastes. From the standpoint of natural reason the writer states, **"All is vanity"** (1:2). It is a picture of the futile repetition of human activity, an endless cycle which, apart from God, does not bring security or meaning to man's life. **"Vanity of vanities"** is the phrase which reoccurs thirty-one times in the book. The author recounts his agonizing search for some contentment, some relief from the relentless empty world he came to inhabit "under the sun." It is the writer's way of speaking of what has happened to man's life, dislodged from God and His divine order; it has become hopelessly empty and meaningless. This is what secularization has given us.

To the existentialist, a courageous person is a person who has shaken off the illusions of any hope and has squarely faced his hopeless reality. The utopian dreams of the previous two centuries crashed and burned. From the blood-soaked trenches of World War One, the horrors of Auschwitz, and the devastation of the atomic bomb of World War Two, there is no divine controller. Our existence is all there is.

The experiences of sensual pleasure and mind-altering drugs created meaning for many people in the 1960s. It was not just a time of long hair, bell bottom trousers and psychedelic drugs. It was an era of upheaval. It was a time characterized by the intellectual and cultural end of modernity's optimism that ushered in a worldview of despair. Godless naturalism had led to the conclusion that life is meaningless. Each person is, therefore, left to make sense of the universe and find meaning on their own. The logical outcome of suspicion of reason and objective truth led to the worldview known as postmodernism.

Postmodernism

Postmodernism states that truth does not exist. Truth is in the eye of the beholder. Truth is what is true to *you*, but there is no such thing as *the* truth. For example, Charles Colson told a story about how he tried to witness to a media personality. Colson told of how his life had changed when he accepted Jesus Christ as his Lord and Savior. The person replied, "Obviously Jesus worked for you." The man continued by telling Colson about someone he knew whose life had been turned around by New Age spirituality. "Crystals, channeling—it worked for her. Just like your Jesus."[6] That's postmodern thinking.

Those who say there is no absolute truth are themselves presenting an absolute truth. It is meaningless and nonsense to say "it is true that there is no truth." Nevertheless, a recent poll showed that 53 percent of those who profess to be Christian do not believe in absolute truth.[7] A person is labeled closed-minded if they believe Jesus is the *only* Way, the *only* Truth and the *only* Light. George Barna, of the Barna Research Group, found that while 60 percent of all Americans believe that the Bible is totally

6 Gene Edward Veith, Jr., *Postmodern Times: A Christian Guide to Contemporary Thought and Culture,* (Wheaton, IL., 1994), pp. 15.
7 *Ibid,* p. 16.

accurate in all of its teachings, 70 percent believe that there are no absolutes.[8] Confusion reigns!

The Enlightenment view is not being rejected because of Christian opposition, but because of postmodern opposition. Christianity's long war and critique of the Enlightenment has left it without a scratch. However, since the 1960s, postmodernism's assaults have brought the Enlightenment world crashing down. Unbelief has usurped unbelief. The overconfident promises of the Enlightenment of creating an ideal world are dead. However, the *premise* on which they were built—freedom from God, authority, the past, and freedom from evil—simply refuse to die. It is these that give strength to the illusion that science can make life better, fueling man's optimism for progress. But why is mankind still enamored with the doctrine of progress when it is so opposed to the facts? Their ideas have been a continual parade of foolishness trying to be passed off as wisdom. For example, Darwin's "pioneering" work has led to increasingly mischievous results. Racism existed long before Darwin; however, he gave racism scientific respectability and apparent justification. His book, *The Origin of Species by Natural Selection*, has as its subtitle, *The Preservation of Favored Races in the Struggle for Life*. Later, in his book *The Descent of Man*, Darwin wrote:

> At some future period, not very distant as measured by centuries, the civilized races of man will almost certainly exterminate and replace the savage races throughout the world. At the same time the anthropomorphous apes...will no doubt be exterminated. The break between man and his nearest allies will then be wider, for it will intervene between man in a more civilized state, as we may hope, even than the Caucasian, and

8 Gary Demar, *Thinking Straight in a Crooked World* (Poder Springs, GA: G.P.Putnam's & Sons, 2001), p.292.

some ape as low as a baboon, instead of as now between the Negro or Australian and the gorilla.[9]

Ideas do have unforeseen consequences. Social Darwinism can easily become militaristic nationalism. Darwin's doctrine of the "preservation of favored races in the struggle for life" eventually led to Nazism and the Jewish holocaust. Henry Morris wrote in his book, *The Long War Against God*, "Nazism was an overripe fruit of the evolutionary tree. So was fascism! And so have been all the other varieties of totalitarianism that have plagued the world since Darwin."[10]

In the twentieth century, riding on the wave of state atheism, the vision of political fascists was the purging of man into "pure man." In psychology, Freudians sought to free man of his deep repressed drives and feelings that had crippled him in order to bring freedom and wholeness to society. Philosophers would provide insight into life and supply a foundation for all sciences. In theology, a "scholarly" approach for the analysis of the Hebrew texts in which the books of Moses were written gave promise of a more modern understanding of the Old Testament. The attitude was that every day, in every way, things were getting better and better. One would think the fires of such foolish illusions would have been extinguished by two world wars. It is ironic how illusions have a way of making short work of reality.

Technopoly

Why does the illusion of progress live on despite the fact the ideologies themselves lay smoldering in the ash heap of history? It is not the ideology that fuels these dreams, it is

9 Charles Darwin, *The Descent of Man*, 2nd ed. (New York, NY: A.L. Burt Co., 1874), p. 178.
10 Henry M. Morris, *The Long War Against God* (Grand Rapids, MI: Baker Book House, 1989), p. 80.

experience founded in technological advances that by and large give science the façade of immortality. It is this that drives the belief in progress. Neil Postman, in his book, *Technopoly,* refers to "the deification of technology, which means that the culture seeks its authorization in technology, finds its satisfaction in technology, and takes its orders from technology. This requires the development of a new kind of social order, and of necessity leads to the rapid dissolution of much that is associated with traditional beliefs. Those who feel most comfortable in Technopoly are those who are convinced that technical progress is humanity's supreme achievement and the instrument by which our most profound dilemmas may be solved."[11] However, progress in manufacturing new things, improving old things of lesser quality, or in developing a better understanding with regards to science is one thing; progress in the human condition is another. And yet there is the tendency to blur the distinction and conclude that if man can make better computers, toaster ovens and television sets then he must be able to make a better self.

Secular Versus Sacred

The idea that the degree of a society's modernization was the degree to which the society ceased to believe in God was true in Europe, but not in America. In Europe, unlike in America, the Enlightenment liberated society of God. America, while heavily secularized, was at the same time very religious. However, religion was banished from public discourse to being a purely private matter. Life was divided into a sacred realm, limited to things like God, values, and morality, and an opposed secular realm, which included science, politics, economics and the rest of one's public life. Religion, then and now, was *not* considered an objective truth, but a personal choice or preference.

---

11 Neil Postman, *Technopoly: The Surrender of Culture to Technology*, (New York, NY: Vintage Books, 1993), p. 71.

It was Francis Schaeffer who best illustrated this concept using the imagery of a two-story building. In the lower story are science and reason. These are considered to be public truth and binding on all people. In the upper story are religion and morals. Another way of putting it is the lower story is facts while the upper story is values or the upper story is subjective while the lower story is objective. The fact/value split enables naturalists to pacify religious people by assuring them that science doesn't totally rule out religious beliefs. However, by exiling those beliefs to the upper story, those beliefs are merely matters of private feelings and not binding truth. Nancy Pearcey in her book, *Total Truth: Liberating Christianity from Its Cultural Captivity,* says this split explains why Christians have so much difficulty in communicating with their culture. Christians don't realize that unbelievers constantly filter what Christians say through a mental fact/value grid.

> "For example, when we state a position on an issue like abortion or bioethics, or homosexuality, *we* intend to assert an objective moral truth important to the health of society—but *they* think we're merely expressing our subjective bias... The fact/value grid instantly dissolves away the objective content of anything we say... To recover a place at the table of public debate, then, Christians must find a way to overcome the dichotomy between public and private, fact and value, secular and sacred. We need to liberate the gospel from its cultural captivity, restoring it to the status of public truth."[12]

Michael Goheen says, "The barred cage that forms the prison for the gospel in contemporary western culture is [the church's] accommodation...to the fact-value dichotomy."[13]

12 Nancy R. Pearcey, *Total Truth: Liberating Christianity from Its Cultural Captivity,* (Wheaton, IL: Crossway Books, 2004), p. 22.

13 Michael Goheen, *"As the Father Has Sent Me, I am Sending You", J.E. Lesslie Newbigin's Missionary Ecclesiology* (Zoetermeer: Uitgeverij Boekencentrum, 2000), p. 377.

The greatest impact of Darwin's theory of evolution was not in his ideas of mutation and natural selection, but more significantly, in the new criteria of what qualifies as objective truth. Darwin's ideas led to a naturalist view of knowledge in which "theological dogmas and philosophical absolutes were at worst totally fraudulent and at best merely symbolic of deep human aspirations."[14] In other words, if Darwinism is true, then religion and philosophical absolutes such as goodness and truth are false. People can still believe in them if they want to, however, they must understand they are "merely symbolic" of human hopes and ideals. Notice the two-story division of truth. Darwinism, according to the naturalistic view of knowledge, is placed in the lower story of public facts, while religion and morality are placed in the upper story of symbols and personal values.

Darwin's Influence

Secularization eventually drove a wedge between science and religion. Christianity and science, for hundreds of years, were thought to be completely compatible and mutually supporting. Most scientists were Christian. The findings of science were hailed as a confirmation, not a challenge to the belief in God. Many scientists such as Copernicus, Kepler, Newton and Galileo believed they were called to use their gifts in praise to God and service to humanity. Their discoveries and inventions were to them a means of reversing the effects of the Fall by alleviating suffering and inconvenience. The final collapse came in the late nineteenth century with Darwin's publication of the theory of evolution. The origin of life was explained in coldheartedly naturalistic terms. Darwin's theory would be the missing piece of the puzzle that completed a naturalistic picture of reality and worldview. It was at this time that science and religion

---

14 Edward A. Percell, *The Crisis of Democratic Theory: Scientific Naturalism and the Problem of Value*, (Lexington, KY: University Press of Kentucky, 1973), pp. 8, 21.

became pitted against each other. Years later in July 1925, in Dayton, Tennessee, the Scopes trial would exemplify this feud in America. John Thomas Scopes was on trial for allegedly teaching evolution in a public school, which was against the law at that time. Instigated by the American Civil Liberties Union, the defendant lost the battle, but eventually won the war. Publicity was given to the evolution issue and in 1965 the law forbidding the teaching of evolution was repealed. Today the tables are turned. The teaching of evolution is allowed to the exclusion of any other view.

Francis Schaeffer believes that the church's ineffectiveness in confronting the culture is because Christians tend to see things in "bits and pieces." Christians focus their concern on the breakdown of the family, abortion, violence in schools, immoral entertainment, etc. They zero in on a wide variety of *individual* issues and fail to see the big picture. They have responded to moral and social decline by embracing political activism. "This heightened activism has yielded good results in many areas of public life, yet the impact remains far less than most had hoped. Why? Because evangelicals often put all their eggs in one basket: they leaped into political activism as the quickest, surest way to make a difference in the public arena—failing to realize that politics tends to reflect culture, not the other way around."[15] Christians may win some legislative victories here and there, but lose the culture. Tragically, they lose their children to the culture. Children raised in Christian homes go to college and abandon their faith. The reason this happens is because they have not been taught how to develop a Christian worldview. "The most effective work...is done by ordinary Christians fulfilling God's calling to reform culture within their local sphere of influence—their families, churches, schools, neighborhoods, workplace, professional organizations, and civic institutions. In order to effect lasting change...we need to develop a Christian worldview."[16]

---

15 Pearcey, *Total Truth*, p. 18.
16 *Ibid*, p. 19.

The decay of the family, attitude toward human life and morality have, as Schaeffer wrote, "come about due to a shift in worldview...to a worldview based on the idea that the final reality is impersonal matter or energy shaped into its current form by impersonal chance."[17] Years before the creation movement, Schaeffer saw that everything hangs on a culture's view of origins. If a society begins with evolution, impersonal forces operating by chance, it will end in naturalism in moral, social and political philosophy.

The conflict of our day, in the ultimate sense, is between theism and naturalism. Theism is the belief that there is a transcendent God who created the universe; naturalism is the belief that natural causes alone are sufficient to explain the existence of everything. The most basic questions are those that reflect the following categories: Is ultimate reality God or the universe? Is there a supernatural realm, or is nature all that exists? Has God spoken and revealed his truth to us, or is truth something we have to discover or create for ourselves? Is there a purpose to our lives, or are we cosmic accidents? All these issues have tremendous implications in counseling.

Charles Darwin's, *The Origin of Species*, hardly mentions the human species. However, the threat to the biblical account of creation and man made in the image of God was clear enough. In the final chapter Darwin simply suggested that, through the study of his theory of evolution, "light will be thrown on the origin of man and his history." He continued by saying, "in the distant future" the study of psychology "will be based on a new foundation."[18] The premise is that natural selection, which accounts for the human body, must also account for all aspects of human belief and behavior.

---

17 Francis Schaeffer, *A Christian Manifesto*, in *The Complete Works of Francis Schaeffer*, vol. 5 (Wheaton, IL: Crossway, 1982), p. 423.

18 Charles Darwin, *The Origin of Species* (New York, NY: Penguin Books, 1968), p. 458.

Chapter Two
After the Funeral: "Unrighteousness"

For the wrath of God is revealed from heaven against all ungodliness and *unrighteousness* of men who suppress the truth in unrighteousness.
Apostle Paul, Romans 1:18
(Italics mine)

On September 11, 2001 two jets left Logan International Airport in Boston, Massachusetts bound for California. Terrorists hijacked the airliners and, a short time later flew them into the twin towers of the World Trade Center in New York City. Two other jets were also hijacked. One plane was flown into the Pentagon in Washington D.C. The other, due to the heroic actions of the doomed passengers, crashed into a field in Pennsylvania. Thousands of people who thought they were beginning just another ordinary day were killed. It was the worst act of terrorism in the history of the United States. The impact and explosion of the planes, the collapsing towers, the chaos, and wreckage would forever be etched in the nation's memory.

In the days that followed, Americans watched uninterrupted television coverage of pictures from the crash scenes. At times, the local and national news reporters would find themselves speechless as they gazed in sad awe at the smoking wreckage that everyone knew hid the crushed and burned bodies of sons, daughters, moms and dads. In contrast to the terrorists' dark hatred was the remarkable courage and tenacity of the rescuers who searched anxiously through mounds of broken concrete and twisted steel. The nation's solidarity was displayed as a huge American flag was draped over the side of the building near the gaping hole at the Pentagon. Throughout the cities and neighborhoods of America, in a gesture of pride and unity, the flag waved in front yards, on car antennas, and store windows. The country was prepared for war.

Immediately following the tragedy something unusual happened. The word 'evil' returned to people's vocabulary. Prior to 9/11 most Americans did not believe in moral absolutes. When God is dead, and there are no enduring standards of right and wrong, people are stripped of their ability to speak of good and evil. Good and evil, in the absence of absolutes, go no deeper than feelings about a particular circumstance whether good or bad. A person may feel and express those feelings by saying, "it was an evil act," or "it was a good act." Evil or good is meaningless except to the individual who feels it was evil or good. But in light of the mass murder of innocent people on 9/11 there was a deep need to speak of what is enduringly, undeniably and eternally wrong. However, since the postmodern conceptual cloud still hung heavily over the country, America had no framework for speaking of evil. The idea of evil remained a cultural and conceptual difficulty. This became increasingly obvious when school teachers were advised by the National Education Association to offer no value judgments to their students on the first anniversary of the 9/11 attack. The business of making moral judgments becomes an impossible task without moral absolutes. Nevertheless, those who claim judgments cannot be made concerning behavior are themselves making a moral judgment.

Life without God

The Enlightenment's confidence in man was only surpassed by its blindness to human corruption. There was a recognition of evil, but it was obscured beneath the optimism of progress which was heralded everywhere. Enlightenment thinkers refused to be shackled by God or any moral authority outside themselves. Postmodern thinkers refuse to be shackled by any objective reality. They point out that different people see the same things differently. Individuals interpret situations differently. What is right for one person may not be right for another. The tendency toward subjectivity—to see things from one's point of view and to conclude their view is true—leads postmodernists to question the objectivity of a person's perception of events, true or false, right or wrong. The skepticism of postmodernists is that truth is a slippery slope. "Uncertainty is the new truth. Doubt and skepticism have been canonized as a form of humility. Right and wrong have been redefined in terms of subjective feelings and personal perspectives."[19] Any truth claims must not be trusted. Paradoxically, despite postmodernism's rejection of objective truth, Darwinism is treated as unquestioned truth. Like modernists, postmodernists believe people are no different from the rest of nature. Unlike modernists, postmodernists are not intolerant of religion, as long as a religion does not make the claim of being *the truth*. Religious exclusivity is unacceptable. From a Christian perspective God, by necessity, reveals truth and so we have doctrine. This idea is loathsome to people today who cast all religions into one melting pot and prefer religious truth to be general.

Once a culture accepts the evolutionary premise, evolutionary explanations of human behavior become a matter of simple logic. The mind evolved and man's behavior arose through adaptation to the environment, in other words, the survival of the fittest. If roses and a candle-light dinner don't result in copulation, then rape or "coercive sex" has evolved as a way of maximizing reproductive success. "That at least some instances of rape are the result of behavioral pathology seems uncontroversial. However, it is far from clear that such a label is appropriate for all cases of rape... The evolutionarily more interesting question is whether rape (or, more generally, coercive sex) has the characteristics of a functional adaptive mating strategy that uses physical aggression as one among

---

19 John MacArthur, *The Truth War*, (Nashville, TN: Thomas Nelson, 2007), p. 16.

many tactics designed to persuade a reluctant partner to mate."[20]
Such an idea is repulsive to most people. To the Darwinist it
is simple logic. Any behaviors that have survived today must
have conferred some evolutionary advantage. If this were not
true, natural selection would have weeded them out years ago.
If one believes that everything evolved, and there is no God,
then evolutionary ethics are inevitable.

Evolution, as expected, flows downhill into moral relativism.
If there is no transcendent truth and nature is all there is, man
is left to construct his own morality. If the here and now is all
there is, then good and bad are arbitrary. Morality is based on or
determined by individual preference or convenience rather than
by necessity or the transcendent nature of a particular attitude
or behavior. Right and wrong are what a person has the courage
to decide for themselves. Carl Henry said, "The first article in
the modern confession of faith is, 'I believe in nature almighty.'
Any world beyond nature is, by presupposition, relegated to the
mythological category. Nature is the 'maker of heaven and earth,
of Jesus Christ, and whatever gods there be,' and is the maker
of reason and morals too, simply because nature is ultimate."[21]

The moral relativism of multiculturalism views all cultures
as morally equivalent. Since there is no transcendent truth, right
and wrong, good and bad, true and false, fall in the limited
perspective of each race, gender, or ethnic group. There is the
African-American perspective, the feminist perspective, the
Hispanic perspective, the homosexual perspective, and so on.
The insistence upon judging certain cultural beliefs and practices
as being morally wrong is unacceptable.

The moral relativism in pragmatism teaches that whatever
works best is right (utilitarianism). A belief is true only if it

20 Louise Barrett, Robin Dunbar, and John Lycett, *Human Evolutionary Psychology*, (Princeton, NJ: Princeton University Press, 2002), p. 266.
21 Carl Henry, *Remaking the Modern Mind*, (Grand Rapids, MI: William B. Eerdmans, 1948), p. 254.

produces desirable results. It is true because it works. William James, one of the most widely read American philosophers, said a belief's "cash value in experiential terms"[22] is all that matters. There is a significant difference between the pragmatic definition of truth and the claim that some truths may be verified or falsified by experience or evidence. The pragmatic view claims that truth *is* what works. James went on to say "On pragmatic principles, if the hypothesis of God works satisfactorily in the widest sense of the word, it is 'true.'"[23] James's point of view said nothing about whether or not there is a God. If God is a useful hypothesis, and has a positive effect upon a person, that's enough.

The fundamental idea of pluralism is cut off from God; man has no point of unity. There is just diversity. There are relatives, but no absolutes, particulars, but no universals. There are many, but there is no unity, no way of bringing the diverse into a coherent whole. The dream of the founders of America was that people of sundry ethnic and religious backgrounds would come to this country from all over the world and become one nation under God. Their belief in a transcendent being, and transcendent truths would be the foundation by which all peoples who came to America would be united. With the death of God there is no transcendent unity. Unity converges upon people's race. There is "unity" among blacks, whites, Hispanics, respectively. A view of tolerance emerges in a pluralistic culture that is different from the virtue of tolerance and longsuffering in the Bible. It is one thing to say all views are tolerated under the laws of the land. It is quite another to say all views are equally valid. Pluralism insists, under the law, that all views are not just equally tolerable, but equally valid. Every view has as much validity as a view that contradicts it. If the preceding statement is true, then truth is destroyed. Truth is impossible. Truth is no

22 William James, *Pragmatism and Four Essays from the Meaning of Truth*, (Cleveland, OH: Meridian, 1967), p. 133.
23 *Ibid.* p. 192.

longer true. Values have no values. Meanings have no meaning. Life is absurd.

German philosopher Friedrich Nietzsche, famous for pronouncing God dead, realized the death of God meant the death of morality. No God, no transcendent standards, and everyone does what is right in their own eyes. He asked the question, "Whither is God?" He answered himself by saying, "I tell you, we have killed him—you and I. All of us are his murderers."[24] Nietzsche was astonished that many people did not comprehend the devastating consequences of the death of God. He knew that if a culture gives up their belief in God they must also give up their biblical ideas of morality and meaning. Nietzsche, as unlikely a prophet as ever was, was right. If man was not created by God, not bound to God's laws, but arose by chance out of the primordial muck, then there are no absolutes and he can do whatever he wants to do. The only intrinsic good, self-justifying end, meaning of life and non-negotiable absolute is pleasing self. Carried to its logical conclusion, a sexual act between unmarried people or partners of the same sex has no moral significance. Nothing has moral significance. However, those who oppose such practices on the grounds they are immoral are themselves called "immoral" in seeking to restrain personal freedoms and the right to privacy. The tables are turned and the righteous are immoral while the immoral are righteous. Light is called darkness and darkness is called light.

Philosophy's blind spot in disavowing God is its unwillingness to admit it has created a monster. No God immediately raises questions of moral law. In colleges and universities across America faculty members, like predators, wait to pounce upon the convictions held by Christian students. Their often repeated, but ill-understood indictment of God concerns the thousands who have been killed in the name of

24 Friedrich Nietzsche, *The Gay Science*, trans. Walter Kaufmann (New York, NY: Random House, 1974), p. 125.

Christianity. However, they never mention the atrocities of unbelievers such as Hitler, Stalin, Mussolini, Mao, Sadam Hussein, etc. They are quick to accuse Christianity but not so eager to blame atheists for their crimes. One thing they have forgotten. The large-scale slaughters at the hands of those atheists were the direct and logical outcome of their godless philosophies. On the other hand, violent actions perpetrated by those who profess to be Christians have been condemned by Jesus Christ Himself.

Sir Arthur Keith, a British anthropologist, atheist, evolutionist and anti-Nazi, drew this chilling conclusion:

> The German Führer, as I have consistently maintained, is an evolutionist; he has consciously sought to make the practice of Germany conform to the theory of evolution.[25]

Viktor Frankl, a survivor of Auschwitz said the Holocaust was the product of atheistic assumptions when he wrote,

> If we present man with a concept of man which is not true, we may well corrupt him. When we present him as an automaton of reflexes, as a mind machine, as a bundle of instincts, as a pawn of drive and reactions, as a mere product of heredity and environment, we feed the nihilism to which modern man is, in any case, prone. I became acquainted with the last stage of corruption in my second concentration camp, Auschwitz. The gas chambers of Auschwitz were the ultimate consequence of the theory that man is nothing but the product of heredity and environment—or, as the Nazis like to say, "of blood and soil." I am absolutely convinced that the gas chambers

25 Arthur Keith, *Evolution and Ethics*, (New York, NY: G.P. Putnam's & Sons, 1947, p. 230.

of Auschwitz, Treblinka, and Maidanek were ultimately prepared not in some ministry or other in Berlin, but rather at the desks and in lecture halls of nihilistic scientists and philosophers.[26]

Evolutionist Richard Dawkins made it clear in a conversation with Jaron Lanier (computer scientist, composer and author), that there is no basis for morality in evolution:

> Jaron Lanier: "There's a large group of people who simply are uncomfortable with accepting evolution because it leads to what they perceive as a moral vacuum, in which their best impulses have no basis in nature."

> Richard Dawkins: "All I can say is, that's just tough. We have to face up to the truth."[27]

Serial killer Jeffrey Dahmer said in an NBC interview:

> If a person doesn't think there is a God to be accountable to, then—then what's the point of trying to modify your behavior to keep it within acceptable ranges? That's how I thought anyway. I always believed the theory of evolution as truth that we all just came from the slime. When we, when we died, you know, that was it, there is nothing …[28]

When Friedrich Nietzsche talked about the darkness that had fallen over mankind, and Russian novelist Fyodor

---

26 Viktor Frankl, *The Doctor and the Soul: Introduction to Logotherapy* (New York, NY.: Knopf, 1982), xxi.

27 Richard Dawkins and Jaron Lanier, "Evolution: The Dissent of Darwin; a Debate", *Psychology Today*, January / February 1997, p. 62.

28 Jeffery Dahmer in an interview with Stone Phillips, *Dateline NBC*, November 29, 1994.

Dostoevski said that when loosed from his Creator's moorings all hell breaks loose, they understood the price tag of the demise of God. Proof positive is our present culture which is adrift in a sea of subjectivity and lawlessness.

At this writing, it has been eight years since the terrorist's attack of 9/11. While Americans were momentarily stunned, they quickly pulled themselves up and built memorials on the site of the Twin Towers, the crash sight in Pennsylvania and the Pentagon. One television commentator said "Americans are survivors. You may knock us down, but we get up twice as big as before." Unfortunately, we cannot say the word "evil" survived 9/11. The fact is the majority of Americans do not believe in the existence of absolute truth. In such uncertainty there is nothing against which to check our thoughts and theories for their veracity. There is no vantage point from which to make a truth or error judgment. Thus we are a culture of moral nomads, ever moving and never stopping. There is no destination. If God does not exist, all things are permissible. Morality vanished with God.

Ungodliness and Unrighteousness

> **For I am not ashamed of the gospel, for it is the power of God for salvation to everyone who believes, to the Jew first and also to the Greek. For in it *the* righteousness of God is revealed from faith to faith; as it is written, "BUT THE RIGHTEOUS *MAN* SHALL LIVE BY FAITH. For the wrath of God is revealed from heaven against all ungodliness and unrighteousness of men who suppress the truth in unrighteousness..."** (Romans 1:16, 17, 18).

"Revealed" is one of the most important words in the Christian faith. Apart from revelation there is no Christianity.

Philosophy talks much about the "quest" for truth, the "search" for reality. The gospel does not invite us to take part in a great search or quest for something. The gospel is an announcement. It is an unfolding, an unveiling. It is a revelation. Paul said that he is not ashamed of the gospel because it is the revelation of God's righteousness.

The gospel, to put it another way, is not a philosophy. It is a statement of a number of facts. It tells of a Person, His death, and the extraordinary claims made by men and women about Him. The world loves philosophy. They love discussing various points of view about reality, human existence, and how we can "know." The gospel is not a system of philosophy and it is this that tends to make the world critical of it. For example, when Paul went to Athens and preached, the Stoics and Epicureans said, "What would this idle babbler wish to say? He seems to be a proclaimer of strange deities..."(Acts 17:18). When Paul began to talk about Jesus Christ's death and resurrection they ridiculed him. They refused to listen to what they considered to be nonsense. While they loved to hear new ideas and alternative perspectives on existing ideas, Paul was not expounding a new philosophical theory. He was talking about a person.

Paul was not ashamed of the gospel because he said it **"is the power of God for salvation..."** The gospel is not *about* the power of God; it *is* the power of God. He equates the gospel itself with God's almighty power. It is truly unique in that it can deliver man from the *guilt* of sin, the *power* of sin, and the *pollution* of sin. It is effective, and will produce God's desired results. It is the "good news" of salvation for all men, the Jew and the Greek. The gospel is about the righteousness of God; God's righteous character and God's righteousness imputed to the sinner through Jesus Christ. It is not some new idea, some new philosophy which may be very interesting and absorbing. No, it is about deliverance from sin, righteousness, and eternal life.

The gospel is set over and against the Greek world. Greek philosophy is great to study, but the tragedy is that philosophy does not get you anywhere. Philosophy tends to begin and end with ideas. It does not save. And so Paul is not ashamed of his message of salvation. It is the most wonderful news that man can hear. If he should go to Rome and be asked to speak in the imperial palace he is ready to do so.

Why was Paul so anxious to preach the gospel in Rome? He did not say it was because he knew many people were living defeated lives and the gospel would give them victory. He did not tell them he was ready to preach the gospel because he had a wonderful experience and he wanted to share it so they too would have a similar experience. He did not talk in terms of the daily struggles that tended to get people down. No, Paul made an amazing statement as to why he was ready to preach the gospel. Paul said, **"For the wrath of God is revealed from heaven…"** Paul did not start with the desires and needs of people. The gospel is not man-centered. It is God-centered. God has been offended. Paul started with the wrath of God and His hatred of sin.

But what has God's wrath been revealed against? Scripture tells us His wrath is **"revealed from heaven against all ungodliness and unrighteousness of men."** Sin is a violation or transgression of God's law, the Ten Commandments. The Ten Commandments are divided into two parts. First, there is reference to man's attitude and relationship toward God. Sin is seen as ungodliness. God said to Moses, **"You shall have no other gods before Me. You shall not make for yourself an idol… You shall not take the name of the LORD your God in vain… Remember the Sabbath day, to keep it holy…"** (Exodus 20:3-11). The second part deals with man's conduct or behavior with regard to behavior in relationship to other people. Unrighteousness is demonstrated in one's failure in their relationship with their neighbors. God said to Moses, **"Honor**

your father and your mother… You shall not murder. You shall not commit adultery. You shall not steal. You shall not bear false witness against your neighbor. You shall not covet your neighbor's house… wife… or anything that belongs to your neighbor" (Exodus 20:12-17). It is important to remember that all sin falls under these two headings. The remainder of Romans chapter one is an exposition and illustration of how mankind is guilty in the matter of ungodliness and unrighteousness. Paul demonstrated how man had deliberately turned from God (ungodliness) and chose unrighteousness, gloried in it, the devastating consequences that followed, and what God did about it.

The essence of all sin is ungodliness. The first sin was ungodliness. Before Adam and Eve ate the fruit from the prohibited tree they had fallen into ungodliness. They doubted God's words. They questioned God's honesty. They set themselves up to be autonomous, to be god. That is ungodliness. Ungodliness has to do with a person's relationship to God. Ungodliness is the refusal to live to worship and praise God only. It is failure to make Him the supreme object of our lives. Jesus said to the lawyer, **"YOU SHALL LOVE THE LORD YOUR GOD WITH ALL YOUR HEART, AND WITH ALL YOUR SOUL, AND WITH ALL YOUR STRENGTH, AND WITH ALL YOUR MIND…"** (Luke 10:27). That is what God expects from us. To fail to love Him like that is ungodly.

Ungodliness and unrighteousness must never be separated. Paul was not writing haphazardly. The order is important. Ungodliness and unrighteousness always go together. Ungodliness is first and unrighteousness second. Not the other way around. Unrighteousness is the consequence of ungodliness. Just as godliness manifests righteousness, ungodliness produces unrighteous behavior. While Adam and Eve maintained their walk with God all was well. When they failed to reject Satan's insinuations against the character of God, they fell into definite acts of transgression. When people forget their relationship to God they forget their conduct and behavior. Those who suggest you can have righteousness, morality or ethics apart from God detract from the glory of God, which is ungodliness. The German philosopher Ernst Haeckel expressed his conviction that you don't need God to have morality when he said,

> ""Convinced that there is no eternal life awaiting him, he [man] will strive all the more to brighten his life on earth and rationally improve his condition in harmony with that of his fellows."[29]

Chapman Cohen, noted orator and writer on behalf of atheistic causes wrote,

> "There is, then, nothing mysterious about the fact of morality. There is no more need for supernaturalism here than there is room for it in any of the arts and sciences. Morality is a natural fact... Morality has nothing to do with God; it has nothing to do with a future life. Its sphere of application and operation is in this world; its authority is derived from the common sense of mankind and is born of the necessities of corporate life."[30]

Nobody has ever discovered a way of having real "morals" without a moral absolute. If there is no moral absolute, we are left with hedonism (doing what we like) or some form of the social contract theory (what is best for society as a whole is right). However, neither of these alternatives corresponds to

---

29 Ernst Haeckel, *The Wonders of Life: A Popular Study of Biological Philosophy*, (New York, NY: Harper and Brothers, 1905), p. 108.

30 Chapman Cohen, article: *Morality Without God*, (American Atheist website, 2006 www.atheists.org/Atheism/Cohen.html , retrieved June, 2007)

the moral notions that men have. Talk to people long enough and deeply enough and you will find that they consider some things are *really* right and some things are *really* wrong. Without absolutes, morals as morals cease to exist, and humanistic man starting from himself is unable to find the absolute he needs. But because the God of the Bible is there, real morals exist. Within this framework I can say one action is right and another wrong without talking nonsense.[31]

Man's sin is inexcusable. Paul said that God's wrath is revealed against all ungodliness and unrighteousness because men **"suppress the truth in unrighteousness."** The general truth about God, not the special truth concerning God's way of salvation, was known to mankind, but man suppressed it, held it down or restrained it. **"For even though they knew God, they did not honor Him as God"** (verse 21). There was a time when man had knowledge of God, but he intentionally suppressed that knowledge and pursued sin. Not only did Paul tell us that man had the knowledge of God, but he went on to explain in detail how man received this knowledge. Paul said, **"Because that which is known about God is evident within them"** (verse 19, italics mine). How is the knowledge of God evident within them? Paul explained, **"For God made it evident *to* them"** (verse 19, italics mine). It is a universal statement. The knowledge of God is available to all mankind. It does not matter how primitive a civilization may be. You will never find a human being, even in the most remote part of the world, who does not have within him a sense of a supreme being. Even the man who professes he is an atheist; even he has a sense of God. This intuitive knowledge of God is the reason an atheist has to argue against God's existence. **"And although they know the ordinance of God, that those who practice such things are worthy of death..."**(v. 32). Paul said "they know." There is in all men a sense of right and wrong. There is a feeling that sin deserves to be judged, will be judged

31 Francis Schaeffer, *The Complete Works of Francis Schaeffer, A Christian Worldview, Vol. 1, A Christian View of Philosophy and Culture, Book One: The God Who is There,* 1982 (Westchester, IL: Crossway Books, 1982), p. 117.

and God is just. Within human nature there is this inevitable "knowing the judgment of God."

Not only has God revealed Himself *within them* (internally), but He has revealed Himself externally in the things which He has made. **"For since the creation of the world His invisible attributes, His eternal power and divine nature, have been clearly seen, being understood through what has been made, so that they are without excuse"** (verse 20). God has revealed Himself in nature. Creation manifests the handiwork of God. He is known by the things He has made—the sun, the moon, the stars and animals. God's "eternal power" can be plainly seen in the design and orderliness of the universe. Either a man believes the whole creation is just an accident or it all has been ordered and arranged by God.

The internal and external knowledge is not sufficient to teach man all he needs to know about God. You will not know the love of God from mountains, valleys, forests and prairies. The heavens declare His glory, but not His anger and hatred of sin. The full moon is not enough to convict a man of his depravity. You will never come to realize His grace and goodness in a sunset. The things which God has made are enough to establish the Being of God, His greatness, His glory, His majesty and His might. They are not enough to save man, but they are enough to render him inexcusable for his godlessness and unrighteousness.

The moral consequences for men and women who exalt their own wisdom and do not glorify God, and do not give Him thanks, are that they turn to vile affection, and horrible perversions. They defend unrighteousness and even say there is something beautiful and good about it. They insist it is not sin. And so evil is defended. However, three times in chapter one Paul declared that, as a result of man's ungodliness, **"God gave them over in the lusts of their hearts to impurity"** (verse 24), **"God gave them over to degrading passions"** (verse 26), and **"God gave them over to a depraved mind"** (verse 28).

Man abandons God, God abandons man. When man refuses to glorify God, dismisses God, throws Him out, God does the exact same thing to man. This is the way God's judgment works. God judicially abandons man. Paul said, **"Receiving in their own persons the due penalty of their error"** (verse 27). The inevitable consequence, the penalty of their error, is moral decline. Man cannot preserve morality without God. When God withdraws His restraining grace and all the corruption within man is loosed, society becomes a hell on earth. Paul summed it up when he wrotc,

> **Being filled with all unrighteousness, wickedness, greed, evil; full of envy, murder, strife, deceit, malice; they are gossips, slanderers, haters of God, insolent, arrogant, boastful, inventors of evil, disobedient to parents, without understanding, untrustworthy, unloving, unmerciful; and although they know the ordinance of God, that those who practice such things are worthy of death, they not only do the same, but also give hearty approval to those who practice them** (Romans 1:29-32).

God Is Dead, What Next?

Once a society turns from God it may take a few generations for the dreadful consequences to become fully manifested. The spiritual and moral fruit of the previous generation may outlive for a time the death of the roots from which it grew. Yet over time, almost undetected, moral laxity or slackness will begin to seep into every corner of society. A "moral vacuum" is created. A vacuum occurs when the air is deliberately sucked out. Systematically God has been sucked out of the heart of the culture. Man's search for absolute morals is doomed to failure. The Absolute is dead. We have outlived Him. In man's search for meaning and morality without God he has effectively lost all three: God, morality and meaning.

Julian Huxley said, "Man is only at the beginning of his period of evolutionary dominance, and that the vast and still undreamt-of possibilities of further advance still lie before him."[32] And while Huxley said, "there is evil in man as well as good,"[33] he was optimistic that man, through continued evolution, is capable of saving himself from evil. Huxley said, "My faith is in the possibilities of man."[34]

It is rather ironic that the denial of God (ungodliness), which has led to an increase in unrighteousness, would produce a bloated sense of confidence in mankind to solve his problems. This is what has happened in our day. This assumption regarding the ability to solve the ills of mankind is what drives the cultural phenomenon of the psychological industry. This is man's attempt to conquer the last enemy. The last enemy is not death, as the Apostle Paul stated, but the disorders and illnesses of our own personalities.

---

32 Julian Huxley, *Religion Without Revelation*, (New York, NY: Mentor, 1957), p. 193.
33 *Ibid.*, p. 196.
34 *Ibid.*, p. 212.

God's Funeral

Chapter Three
Connecting the Dots: Ungodliness, Unrighteousness and Bad Feelings

O Lord, rebuke me not in Your wrath, and chasten me not in Your burning anger. For Your arrows have sunk deep into me, and Your hand has pressed down on me. There is no soundness in my flesh because of Your indignation; there is no health in my bones *because of my sin*. For my iniquities are gone over my head; as a heavy burden they weigh too much for me. My wounds grow foul *and* fester *because of my folly*.

David, Psalm 38:1-5 (italics mine)

The culture in which we live takes feelings and emotions very seriously. Nearly every problem, difficulty or hardship of life is considered a threat to our emotional well-being. Everyday disappointment, failure or rejection is regarded as a risk to one's self-esteem. "Vulnerable," "emotionally scarred," "stressed," "traumatized," "having hurts" or "issues" is the language of emotionalism that pervades politics, the workplace, schools, universities, churches and everyday life. This is how, through the grid of emotion, that contemporary culture makes sense of man.

Therapeutic language is used not only to describe an individual's state of emotion; it is also used to describe a nation's state of emotion. Following the attacks on the World Trade Center and Pentagon on September 11, 2001, words like "time of *national* trauma" and "*nation* in distress" were commonly used to describe the atmosphere. Sociologist Neil Smelser said the events of 9/11 inflicted *"cultural* trauma on America."(Italics mine)[35] Following Timothy McVeigh's conviction for bombing the federal building in Oklahoma City, the words "healing" and "closure" were the most commonly used expressions by those interviewed. Words like "healing" and "closure" are words that express finality, comfort and relief. They are essentially psycho-medical concepts.

Plagued by uncomfortable feelings as a result of ungodliness and unrighteousness, man finds himself alone. There is no God. Nature is our creator. There is nothing out there. Just silence. There is only self. While man has freed himself, at least in his mind, from God, he has imprisoned himself in a lonely and meaningless universe, a place where meaning is that which man himself assigns to something. In the past, man understood himself in the context of having been created in the image of God. For centuries that was the language of self-understanding. "Made in God's image and likeness" enabled people, in spite of their outward differences in culture, gender, age, education and occupation, to view humanity as being the same in all places and at all times. While the exact nature and meaning of the image of God has been debated within the various Christian traditions, there has never been any doubt that human beings are more than a conglomeration of genes, electrical impulses and chemicals; more than the products of their environment and circumstances; more than their gender and ethnicity; and more than machines consuming products. People are spiritual beings. However, in our secularized culture we perceive ourselves only as material beings. When God died, not only did everything around us lose meaning, but we lost meaning. We have been demoted from humans made in the image of God to animals. We are spiritual beings, but we do not know it. Life revolves around self. Self is all that remains. The old spiritual quest, love God and neighbor, has been abandoned and replaced by

---

35 See www.as.wvu.edu/carlsonprofessorship/Smelser 17 September 2002.

newer quests for self-discovery, fulfillment and psychological wholeness.

Capitalism provides self with abundance; markets are flooded with goods and endless ways of entertainment. America has become a paradise of unlimited consumption where desire becomes the substitute for moral norms. Without God, all that's left is what *you* want; doing what is right and desirable in *your* eyes. Desire *is* the norm; the endless pursuit of wants is evidence the rules of the past no longer apply. Man, because that's all there is, is living for *himself*.

The here and now is all there is and a culture of plenty leads people to define life in terms of possessions, feelings and experiences. We are what we have or what we feel. Our wants become needs and luxuries become necessities. The fact that man's ingenuity has created an abundance of things along with untamed desires is proof we have moved from a traditional to a modern society, from a time when God was a natural part of life, to one in which God is not. In the days of our parents and grandparents what people wanted was limited because there were limited choices. Their view of life and their experiences were restricted. To the average American there were no fabulous vacations, Caribbean cruises, timeshares, exotic perfumes, luxury automobiles, theme parks, or fitness clubs. Wants were not needs and luxuries were not necessities.

Today, products are not purchased merely for our use, but to improve sex appeal, elevate status, take away boredom or raise self-esteem. Consuming is essential to the nurture of the self. It is all about self and self-improvement. Today's self, no longer in the image and likeness of God, is creating its own image. "Image management" has become a lucrative business. The preoccupation with how things appear on the outside has replaced substance. Traditional values and self-denial are undermined and an ethic of hedonism, the belief that good and evil are defined in terms of pleasure and pain, takes its place. Robert Bork, Supreme Court nominee, wrote about the decline of morals in contemporary society. He said that "the traditional virtues of this culture are being lost, its vices multiplied, its values degraded – in short, the culture itself is unraveling."[36]

The idea that our society is sliding deeper and deeper into moral decline is no longer arguable. It is a given fact, stripped of any divine meaning; America has lost its moral center. We have become autonomous and life is recast in psychological terms. Self is all that remains when God has disappeared. At the core of this moral change is the conviction that self-gratification is a right. Self-restraint, once the cardinal virtue, has given way to self-gratification, the new cardinal virtue. The ethic of self—what is right for me—is the external standard. We have lost sight that we are moral beings shaped in the image and likeness of God. We are animals surviving. We are a law unto ourselves. There is no moral map to guide man along his way through life. There is no map at all. Self-interest has taken the place of divine intervention. Evil becomes commonplace and ordinary. Sin is called sickness. This in turn leads to feelings of depression, anxiety, fear, guilt, etc., and thus, in order to deal with feelings, society takes on a psychological mindset. Today people instinctively turn to psychological cures as they once turned to God.

Dis-ease and Psychology

Sin and judgment in a moral world are replaced in a psychologized world by sickness and "understanding." In order to quiet the dis-ease caused by ungodliness and unrighteousness, man has invented a plethora of "healing" theories and therapies. With therapeutic warmth and acceptance, value-free diagnoses are made of the client's wounds and hurts. Sin is domesticated in order to support secular notions about the self. This practice

36 Robert H. Bork, *The Hard Truth About America*, *The Christian Activist* #7

pervades the church. What a culture believes about self is closely related to what they believe about God. As righteousness fades, so the view of God's holiness, as part of His transcendence, fades. God, "a feeling Father," is predominately portrayed in terms of the positive ways He serves man by relieving him of his nervousness, depression or poor self-image rather than His moral character. This is very appealing to modern congregations since they too are preoccupied with their feelings and emotions.

In a culture where there is no transcendent reference point outside of man, sin becomes unreal, abstract, a conceptual impossibility. However, life is confusing and difficult to explain because man sins. Psychological explanations, calling sin sickness, are invented to explain bad feelings like depression, anxiety and guilt. Man is on a merry-go-round. He passes "ungodliness." Around he travels passing "unrighteousness," "bad feelings," and then comes full circle back to "ungodliness." He is without a moral framework. Buying a car, robbing a convenience store, helping a woman change a flat tire, aborting a baby are just pieces of information or experiences. They have no meaning except what man himself assigns to them. There is no way of knowing which one is important or trivial, good or bad, true or false. A feeling of guilt in a postmodern therapeutic world makes no sense because there is no transcendent accountability. Guilt is a neurosis to be treated with therapy. Dis-ease, the result of ungodliness and unrighteousness, is disease.

Besieged by depression, anxiety, a sense of discontent and inner emptiness, the "psychological man" seeks serenity of mind in ideas that increasingly perpetuate his disturbing moods and feelings. Psychologists are his main allies in his struggle for equilibrium. In them he hopes to find the modern equivalent of salvation—"mental health." However, the materialistic perspective that the human body is a biological machine, and not a vessel given by God to house the immortal soul, makes psychological wholeness elusive. He defines himself, dehumanizes himself, as a bundle of chemical reactions. He is not made in God's image. He is an evolutionary accident. He is an animal that feels bad and is trying to feel better.

Psychology's influence, like a soaking rain, has reached down into the roots of people's lives. Ironically, while it has lent its "expertise" to the criminal justice system, it nevertheless preaches blame or guilt as being destructive to the human personality. Historian Gertrude Himmelfarb said the aversion of psychology to make moral judgments "is now so firmly entrenched in the popular vocabulary and sensibility that one can hardly imagine a time without it."[37] Morality is considered to be a repressive force that stifles human progress. The goal of therapy is to emancipate clients from such backwardness of morality and the guilt it fosters. Harry Emerson Fosdick, preacher and counselor, wrote, "Moral ideals, stiff, rigid, and promiscuously applied, can do incalculable harm."[38] And so, morality is viewed with suspicion, especially when it is associated with obligations, since one's supreme obligation is said to be toward self. Ungodliness is perpetuated by psychology.

Ungodliness, Unrighteousness and Bad Feelings

Every model of counseling has its own doctrine of man. In other words, why do people do what people do and how can you help them change? Since the Bible asks and answers the same question, every model of counseling is put in competition with God's Word.

According to the Bible, mankind was created and given spiritual and physical life to live in communion with and reflect the character of God. However, through unbelief, self-will and pride, man fell into a sinful condition. C.S. Lewis said as a result

---

37 Gertrude Himmeelfarb, *The De-moralization of Society: From Victorian Virtues to Modern Values* (New York, NY: Vintage, 1994), p. 12.

38 Cited in Starker, *Oracle*, p. 55.

of the Fall "man is now a horror to God and to himself and a creature ill-adapted to the universe, not because God made him so but because he has made himself so by the abuse of his free will."[39] Man was created good and has become bad. Science, so called, says they have proven the contrary. Instead of man having fallen out of a state of virtue and innocence, he has slowly raised out of brutality and savagery.

God's purpose is that man's whole life emanate from a personal relationship with Him. Biblical solutions to life's problems lie within that relationship. When one deals with emotional-behavioral problems from a psychological perspective rather than or in addition to a spiritual perspective, confusion arises. To integrate biblical truth that teaches man is born in sin with, for example, Carl Roger's model that says man is intrinsically good, is misleading and confusing. Until man is redeemed by Jesus Christ, indwelt by the Holy Spirit, he is fallen. All other models avoid the question concerning the fallen condition, the propensity of man to sin and Christ's redeeming work. Contrary to Otto Rank, man's problems are not due to birth order, nor are man's difficulties explained, as Sigmund Freud did, by unconscious processes or Abraham Maslow's hierarchy of needs such as self-esteem. Problems of living, because they involve the fallen or redeemed condition of man, are basically spiritual in nature. Man was not created to live independent from God. Man was created to live in active, obedient dependence on God. Therefore, it is a serious error to approach problems of living as though they are not related to the spirit.

All counseling issues—anger, bitterness, worry, drunkenness, greed, adultery, disobedience to parents, etc.—are spiritual issues. They are not "health" issues; they are "heart" issues. Jesus said, **"For out of the heart proceed evil thoughts, murders,**

---

39 C.S. Lewis, *The Problem of Pain* (New York, NY: HarperCollins Publisher, 1996), p. 63.

adulteries, fornications, thefts, false witness, blasphemies" (Matthew 15:19, NKJV). The heart drives behavior, thus Scripture warns men to watch over their heart **"for out of it spring the issues of life"** (Proverbs 4:23, NKJV). For counseling to be truly Biblical in nature, and please God, it must be directed at changing the heart and not merely modifying behavior. The Pharisees were behavior modificationists. They prayed at the designated times, tithed and gave alms to the poor. However, Jesus said, their hearts were far from Him.

The problems people face may not always be the result of their sin; they may be the result of someone else's sin. However, all problems are the result of living in a sinful world. The Bible clearly teaches that a counselee's experiences are a means of bringing him closer to God. Since moving closer to God is the single most important aspect of change, it must be the primary focus in counseling. Of the nearly three hundred theories about man and his problems only Genesis 3 provides the real information as to the source of man's problems and difficulties.

Adam and Eve had sinned. In the cool of the day when God normally walked and communed with them, Adam and Eve, out of fear ran and hid from God. The openness they once enjoyed no longer existed. Sin had driven a wedge between man and his Creator, yet God lovingly sought after them. At long last, filled with a sense of shame, they emerged from their hiding place. When God confronted Adam he did not repent, but immediately began to make excuses.

Beginning with Adam and down through the history of mankind the fundamental sinful response pattern has been to avoid responsibility by blaming someone or something else. Avoiding responsibility is characteristic of all non-biblical models of counseling. Skinnerians insist man is controlled by an impersonal environment. According to Freud man is controlled by an irrational unconscious. Responsibility is attacked and blame is shifted to so-called chemical imbalances, low self-esteem and so on. Man's uniqueness, made in the image of God, is undermined. He is dehumanized. Animals are not responsible to love God and neighbor. There is no God-given moral law for animals. This universal tendency is described by Jesus in the *Parable of the Great Supper*. Jesus said, **"*all* alike began to make excuses"** (Luke 14:18, italics mine). Adam pointed his finger at Eve and proclaimed his innocence, by condemning her and even God Himself. Adam said, **"The woman whom *you* gave to be with me, *she* gave me, and I ate"** (Genesis 3:12, italics mine). Then God asked Eve, "What is this you have done?" Eve replied, **"The serpent deceived me, and I ate"** (Genesis 3:13). With this, a wedge was not just driven between Adam and God, but between Adam and his wife. Herein is the seed of every major problem. Adam did not express any sorrow for his sin. He did not repent or assume responsibility. Instead he shifted the blame and excused himself. All blame-shifting amounts to running and hiding from God.

Adam's rebelliousness and refusal to repent led to feelings of guilt and shame. "Feelings follow behavior" is a principle found first in Genesis 3 and throughout the entire Bible.

The Bible teaches that there is a relationship between behavior and feelings. Ungodliness leads to unrighteousness which leads to guilt, depression, anxiety, fear, shame, etc. After they had eaten of the forbidden fruit, Adam and Eve fled from the presence of God because they were "afraid" (Genesis 3:10). When God rejected Cain's offering he became angry and depressed. God asked Cain, **"Why are you angry? And why has your countenance fallen?"** God said to Cain **"If you do well, will not *your countenance* be lifted up?"** (Genesis 4:6-7). If Cain would change his behavior his feelings would change. God's rhetorical question to Cain sets forth the important principle that behavior determines feelings.

Even so, not all bad feelings such as depression and not all sicknesses are the result of a person's sin or sinful habits. Jesus' disciples asked about a man who was born blind, **"Rabbi, who sinned, this man or his parents, that he would be born blind?"** Jesus responded, *"It was* **neither** *that* **this man sinned, nor his parents; but it was so that the works of God might be displayed in him"** (John 9:1-3).

The Bible clearly teaches there are three causes of problems such as bad or uncomfortable feelings (depression, anxiety, fear, etc.) and disease. The causes are organic, demon possession, and sin. Hypothyroidism may cause depression, however, if an organic cause cannot be found it may be related to the person's behavior. There is no other cause such as so-called mental illness. In the ultimate sense, all sickness is traced to Adam's sin. Yet the Bible does acknowledge an immediate relationship between sin, bad feelings and sickness. Jesus said to a man He had healed, **"Behold, you have become well; do not sin anymore, so that nothing worse happens to you"** (John 5:14). Jesus' words implied that the man's original sickness came from sin. The Lord then warned him not to continue in his sin lest a worse judgment come upon him. Another example is found in 1 Corinthians 11:30. The Lord's Supper was being abused in the church at Corinth. Some believers, by failing to discern the Lord's body (NKJV wording), were eating and drinking judgment upon themselves. Paul said **"For this reason many among you are weak and sick, and a number sleep"** in other words, died. Judgment on either a believer or unbeliever may come in this life and bad feelings or sickness may be God's means for bringing that judgment (1 Corinthians 11:30, 31).

Medicating the Problem

With God out of the way, and an anthropology that states man is good, people misunderstand uncomfortable feelings. Bad feelings, resulting from sinful behavior and attitudes, are reinterpreted as being symptoms of sickness. People who are anxious, depressed or angry often talk about having "emotional problems." While their emotions may not be very pleasant, their problem is not their emotions. Their emotions are working fine, that's why they feel the way they feel. Their problem is their behavior. Medicating behavior may relieve the feeling of depression or anxiety, but it does not address the cause, i.e. the behavior. The focus must be on the behavior that causes the feeling.

For Christians, guilt, worry, fear, anxiety, depression, anger and many other non-organic uncomfortable feelings or bothersome emotions are simply human or fleshly avoidance responses to failures to heed God's conviction for some sin or a pattern of sin. Alternatively, they may be the work of the Holy Spirit directly, as He strives to get our attention. What then can be said about the use of psychoactive medications in the treatment of these non-organic feelings and emotions? How can we draw a parallel between God's Word and medication use? Clearly the medications available today can lift depression, reduce anxiety, blunt guilt, stabilize mood, control angry outbursts and make us *feel* better. Quite simply, dare we only address feelings when heart issues are the central problem? Dare we act to chemically dull the work of the Holy Spirit? Dare we quiet that still small voice of internal conviction and risk external affliction or worse?[40]

People feel badly because of bad behavior. The relationship between feelings and behavior is taught throughout the Bible. The prophet Ezekiel said that people who behave sinfully will loathe themselves (20:43). The book of Proverbs clearly teaches that feelings flow from behavior. For example:

My son, give attention to my words; incline your ear to my sayings. Do not let them depart from

40 David Tyler and Kurt Grady, *Deceptive Diagnosis: When Sin is Called Sickness* (Bemidji, MN: Focus Publishing, 2006), pp. 97-98.

your sight; keep them in the midst of your heart. For they are life to those who find them, and health to all their body (Proverbs 4:20-22).

David understood well the connection between behavior and feelings when he wrote:

> **There is no soundness in my flesh because of your indignation; there is no health in my bones *because of my sin*. For my iniquities are gone over my head; as a heavy burden they weigh too much for me. My wounds grow foul and fester because of my folly** (Psalm 38:3-5, italics mine).

Peter, quoting 1 Peter 3:10, points out that good living produces good feelings:

> **The one who desires life, to love and see good days, must keep his tongue from evil and his lips from speaking deceit.**

The correlation between feelings and behavior is seen in David's son, Amnon, and his sinful desires for his half-sister Tamar:

> **Now it was after this that Absalom the son of David had a beautiful sister whose name was Tamar, and Amnon the son of David loved her. Amnon was so frustrated because of his sister Tamar that he *made himself ill*, for she was a virgin, and it seemed hard to Amnon to do anything to** her (2 Samuel 13:1-2, italics mine).

Peter addressed the importance of good behavior relating to a good conscience when he wrote:

> **...and keep a good conscience so that in the thing in which you are slandered, those who**

reviled your good behavior in Christ will be put to shame (1 Peter 3:16).

When man sins, he feels it. Jay Adams wrote:

> A good conscience, according to Peter depends upon good behavior.   Good lives come from good deeds; good consciences come from good behavior. Conscience, which is man's ability to evaluate his own actions, activates unpleasant visceral and other bodily warning devices when he sins. "When he fails he feels it." These responses serve to alert him to the need for correction of the wrong behavior which the conscience would not tolerate. Bad feelings are the red light on the dashboard flashing out at us, the siren screaming at high pitch, the flag waving in front of our faces. Visceral discomfort is a God-structured means of telling human beings that they have violated their standards.[41]

A person's conscience, depending upon his behavior, will either accuse him or defend him. Paul wrote to the Christians at Rome:

> **For when Gentiles who do not have the Law do *instinctively* the things of the Law, these, not having the Law, are a law to themselves, in that they show the work of the Law written in their hearts, *their conscience bearing witness* and their thoughts alternately accusing or else defending them...** (Romans 2:14-15, italics mine).

Many believers fail to connect sin with the misery that brings them to counseling. A person's depression may be the result of

---

41 Jay Adams, *Competent to Counsel,* (Grand Rapids, MI. Zondervan Publishing House, 1970), p.94.

their bitterness, anger or unwillingness to grant forgiveness to someone. Their feelings of anxiety may be due to their immoral behavior or thoughts. The Bible says **"Do not be deceived, God is not mocked; for whatever a man sows, this he will also reap"** (Galatians 6:7). The laws of God are not optional. Believers or unbelievers, it does not matter, cannot violate them without suffering consequences. The law of gravity is not optional. If a person violates the law of gravity the consequences can be tragic.

God made man with the capacity to experience pain. He also placed in the spirit of man the capacity for triggering painful emotions such as guilt, depression, anxiety, fear, etc. These negative emotions have a positive function. They are only perceived as being negative because they are distressing. However, as Jesus said, tribulation works to makes us like Him. Physical pain is what brings individuals to physicians' offices. Physical pain can therefore be a positive thing. It warns us that there is something wrong. In the same way, counselees do not seek counseling unless there is some kind of emotional distress. Emotional "pain" should likewise be viewed as a warning that there is something wrong.

A Science of the Mind

The psychological mindset that pervades our culture did not just appear from nowhere. It took off as a result of a one hundred year long expansion of the influence of psychology. By the end of the nineteenth century, there was a considerable interest in this new profession's claim to provide a science of the mind. Its popularity and status steadily grew during the first half of the twentieth century. By the late 1960s, psychology had become a significant feature in mainstream America. Liberated from the Judeo-Christian tradition, the therapeutic ethos emancipated man which enabled him to "be all he could be." Responsibility was the goal, but it was not responsibility to God, but to self.

The promise of psychology was autonomy. It was autonomy from tradition. Tradition no longer provided a standard for making sense of life. Shared values and meaning dissipated. Meaning became intensely personal. "What does such and such mean to you?"

Ungodliness and unrighteousness led to bad feelings, thus creating a demand for psychological answers for those bad feelings as opposed to biblical ones. It was believed that the psychotherapeutic ideology would provide that certainty as well as create a moral climate apart from transcendent meaning. It would offer a moral solidarity in the form of psychological solidarity. The goal was autonomy from tradition, from God, but not from the therapist. Under the therapist's guidance, the uncomfortable feelings (depression, anxiety, fear, guilt, etc.) that are the result of ungodliness, unrighteousness, or sin, are reinterpreted using psychopathological terms. By the mid 1980s, the therapeutic tenet that stated all problems stem from psychological causes was firmly planted in the minds of Americans.

God's Funeral

Chapter Four
Living with the Canaanites

When the angel of the LORD spoke these words to all the sons of Israel, the people lifted up their voices and wept. So they named that place Bochim; and there they sacrificed to the LORD.

Judges 2:4, 5

God had delivered His people from the bondage and servitude of Egypt. He brought them to the Jordon River, parted the waters, and they marched into the land God had promised their fathers. God decreed the destruction of the inhabitants, the Canaanites, a race of people loathsome in God's sight, and appointed Israel as their executioners. However, Israel did not do as God commanded. Israel felt God's command was too severe. They reasoned, as we all tend to do right before we intentionally disobey God, that God Himself is merciful and kind. Surely God would not be angered if they treated the Canaanites with tolerance and kindness. Perhaps they could even learn something of the civilization of the Canaanites. The Canaanites were an advanced people. The Israelites could study their arts and sciences. They could go to their temples and see the gods they worshipped. They said to the Canaanites, "Let us be neighbors and live together."

Israel's tolerance led to imitation and they soon fell into the ways of the Canaanites. They became a mixed race. They became as vile as the heathens they conquered. Laxity turned into mischief as the children of Jehovah worshipped at the altar of Baal. It got worse as they bowed before the unclean goddess, Ashtaroth. It wasn't long before the deities and demons of the Canaanites crowded out all of their devotion and remembrance of Jehovah. Ungodliness led them down the road to unrighteousness and lewdness. Finally, they were indistinguishable from the nation in which they dwelt.

God sent an angel to admonish and preach repentance to the children of Israel. The angel reminded them of the mercies and goodness of God over the years. He scolded them for their rebellion and warned them of the judgment that would come. When the angel had finished, the people were greatly distressed. They wept and called the place Bochim, or the place of weepers.

One would think their tears and sacrifice to the Lord were good signs. However, it is plain they were not penitent tears, but tears caused by their anticipation of coming judgment. They were the tears of those who did not want to give up the sin they loved, but dreaded the consequences. When repentance is true, it is practical. If the Israelites had truly turned to God, they would have turned from their sin and God would not have judged them. They wept because the Canaanites would rule them.

Affected by the Culture

We are all greatly affected by our culture and people around us. The impulse to "fit in" is hard to resist, especially in a direction pleasing to our fallen nature. Israel found they were alone among other nations. They worshipped Jehovah whom they could not see, while their neighbors practiced gorgeous rites and mystic ceremonies. This tempted them to set up idols of their own.

Our natural inclination to focus on the visible is why psychology is so tempting. It offers us theories and therapies founded on "science." It appears to be more concrete and substantial. However, the materialistic explanations lead us to place greater and greater reliance upon man and less and less upon God. It interprets the difficulties of living in a way that destroys our ability to see God working in our lives. Just like the Israelites, the more enamored and immersed in the ideas and practices of psychology we become, the less of a role God plays in the practical and everyday events of our lives.

The prevailing belief among Christians is that psychology is a discipline founded on scientific research, that it is value-neutral and contains elements of truth beneficial to us. Lee Coleman, a psychiatrist who has testified in over one hundred courtroom trials, said that his job was "to educate the judge or jury about why the opinions produced by these professionals [psychologists and psychiatrists] have no scientific merit."[42] Psychiatrist Thomas Szasz wrote, "the clever and cynical destruction of the spirituality of man, and its replacement by a positivistic 'science of the mind...' is not merely a religion that pretends to be a science [but] a fake religion that seeks to destroy true religion."[43] William James said over a hundred years ago, "I wish by treating psychology as a science to help her become one."[44] Psychiatrist E. Fuller Torrey wrote, "The techniques used by western psychiatrists are, with few exceptions, on exactly the same scientific plane as the techniques used by witchdoctors." Psychology is not a science.

Israel believed that by sparing the Canaanites, their tolerance would be beneficial. They could learn from the Canaanites and the Canaanites could learn from them. They "naively" entered into treaties, but their unholy compromise proved pride does go before the fall. The same careless practice and naïve attitude is common in the church today. We have convinced ourselves we can coexist with the enemies of Christ and not be affected by

42 Lee Coleman, *The Reign of Terror,* (Boston, MA, Beacon Press, 1984), p. xii-xv.
43 Thomas Szasz, *The Myth of Psychotherap,y* (New York, NY, Doubleday, 1978), p. xxiv.
44 William James, *Collected Essays and Reviews*, 1920, "A Plea for Psychology as a Natural Science," 1972, p. 8.

their ways. We foolishly and arrogantly believe we will glean only their "wisdom" and shun their errors, believing that, after all, "all truth is God's truth." We are not weak and gullible like the Israelites. They were foolish, but we are wise.

Is "all truth God's truth," as Christian integrationists tell us, or is that one of Satan's lies intended to justify the use of atheistic theories in "Christian psychology"? The writer of the Psalms was surely not referring to science or psychology when he wrote, **"His truth *shall be thy* shield and buckler"** (91:4, KJV). Paul was not referring to science or mere facts when he wrote; **"Stand firm therefore, HAVING GIRDED YOUR LOINS WITH TRUTH"** (Ephesians 6:14). God's truth is revealed by the Holy Spirit to God's people. Jesus said to Pilate, **"You say *correctly* that I am a king. For this I have been born, and for this I have come into the world, to testify to the truth. Everyone who is of the truth hears My voice"** (John 18:37). God's truth is not the same as facts. Facts, such as the sky is blue, the earth is round, light travels at 186,000 miles per second or George Washington was our first president, are available to all people. The truth which sets us free is only known to the followers of Jesus Christ. Something may be factually true, but it is not "the truth" of which the Bible speaks.

A lot of "scientific" facts Christian psychology likes to promote under the umbrella of "all truth..." are not science, or facts at all. For example, Freud's id, ego and superego are not science or fact (you can cut open a cadaver and look for an id, ego and superego, but you will never find them). Anger as a disease is not science or fact. Christian psychology tries to lump everything that is true into Jesus' words about "truth." Something may be scientifically or historically true but it is not *the truth* and cannot be part of it. The truth Jesus spoke of was not facts available to all people but truth only available to believers. Jesus said **"My sheep hear MY voice"** (John 10:27). **Truth is revealed by the Holy Spirit who is called the Spirit of**

Truth." Jesus said, **"I am the way, and the truth…"** (John 14:6). Jesus did not mean that God's Word is factual or that it contains *part* of the truth that is found elsewhere. He said He was *The Truth*.

The sufficiency of Scripture is denied in the phrase "all truth is God's truth." This phrase is commonly used to justify looking outside of the Bible to atheists for more of "God's truth." Christian psychology claims Jesus wasn't claiming that His Word was the *only* truth. They believe Jesus left the door open for other sources of truth. There is a big difference between temporal truth (science / history) and the truth of God. Jesus clearly stated that unbelievers cannot receive God's truth. Jesus said, **"The Spirit of truth, whom the world cannot receive"** (John 14:17). It is deceptive to promote the theories of Sigmund Freud, Carl Rogers and others as being part of God's truth.

Many believers have arduously studied the theories of psychology. Few have made any effort to familiarize themselves with the critique of psychology by a small, but intellectually impressive group of individuals, one being Thomas Szasz. Szasz, a psychiatrist, gained his reputation as one of psychiatry's foremost critics of the mental health system. In 1961 Szasz, in his book, *The Myth of Mental Illness,* said mental illnesses do not exist. The mind, unlike the brain which is part of the material body, is an immaterial entity and therefore, it is impossible for it to be afflicted by illness. Szasz did not deny that people who were considered mentally ill were suffering. He denied that they were suffering from a disease of the mind. Instead Szasz said they were suffering from "problems of living." [45]

In the same way, R.D. Laing gained his reputation as a critic of the mental health system. While most of their colleagues fell in step with the popular notions of mental illness, Szasz and

---

45 Thomas Szasz, *The Myth of Mental Illness,* (New York: Hocher, Harpers, 1961), pp. x-xii.

Laing questioned the idea. The psychological concept rested on the premise that the social order itself was conducive to happiness. People who have problems are people who have trouble "adjusting" and are discontent or mentally ill. Laing insisted that social order, or the world in and of itself, did not promote happiness. He was convinced that there was something essentially wrong with the world. Laing's position was in accord with Christianity. The Christian position judges the world by a higher standard, God's Word. The Apostle Paul wrote, **"And do not be conformed to this world, but be transformed by the renewing of your mind, so that you may prove what the will of God is, that which is good and acceptable and perfect"** (Romans 12:2). Clearly, Paul did not believe a sign of spiritual well-being or mental health was adjustment to this world. Paul said, **"For the wisdom of this world is foolishness before God. For it is written, '*He is* THE ONE WHO CATCHES THE WISE IN THEIR CRAFTINESS'"** (1 Corinthians 3:19). The psychological mindset, "the wise," does not bring people into conformity with Jesus Christ, but conformity with the world. Adjusting to this world was never our Lord's goal for us.

Down the street from Gateway Biblical Counseling and Training Center where I am the director, is another counseling center that advertises in bold letters, "Christian Psychology." While there is Freudian psychology, Rogerian psychology and so on, there is no such thing as Christian psychology. We do not talk about Christian dentistry, carpentry or optometry. There is Freudian psychology, Jungian, Adlerian, Humanistic, Behavioristic, but you will never find in any university or public library a listing for Christian psychology. No prophet or apostle founded "Christian psychology." The words Christian and psychology are opposites. If a counselor is a Christian then he or she should not use psychology. If the counselor uses psychology, then he or she should not use the Bible. Christian psychology is an oxymoron. They are incongruous and incompatible words, like "cruel kindness" or "jumbo shrimp."

In a paper presented at the Western Association of Christians for Psychological Studies, psychologists J. Suthermand and P. Poelstra said, "We are often asked if we are 'Christian psychologists' and find it difficult to answer since we don't know what the question implies. We are Christians who are psychologists, but at the present time there is no acceptable Christian psychology that is markedly different from non-Christian psychology."

Nevertheless, there are hundreds of authors and church leaders who call themselves and are known as Christian psychologists. Christian psychology is one of the most popular subjects in Christian universities and seminaries. However, the content of the programs and courses must be approved for accreditation by the American Psychological Association, an organization consisting of mostly unbelievers and atheists.

One is left to ponder these days the way we put words together and describe things. Coupling the words Christian and psychology sounds right in our culture and church. So why not promote Jesus alongside of psychology? What damage will be done by putting Jesus Christ alongside Sigmund Freud or Alfred Adler on the marquee or sign? This is a particularly modern way of doing things. Polar opposites displayed together. In our culture, the one validates the other. In reality, the one nullifies the other.

In our culture and church the words Christian and psychology when linked together are ordinary and usual. We have grown accustomed to seeing them together. Christ-centered Freudianism, or Rogerianism makes some cringe while others believe it is a valuable and useful relationship. The reason these two words sound normal can only be understood in the context of the changes which have occurred over the past century. These changes have been inconspicuous; nevertheless, every nook and cranny of our society has been flooded with change. The changes have not merely been in technology, education, politics or economics, but have been intensely theological and spiritual. It is a change not just outwardly, but inwardly. It is change at the very core of our being where meaning is interpreted. *We have changed!*

The church has been ingesting heavy doses of psychology for decades. We have adopted their "wisdom" and attempted to sanctify it by calling it Christian counseling or Christian psychology. We tolerate that which God despises. We visit the temples of the psychological way and bow before their man-gods. We have replaced biblical insights into our behaviors and moods with human design. Secularism is now setting the terms of how Christians approach grief, depression, and the seemingly endless numbers of problems life brings their way. When Israel failed to destroy the Canaanites and their gods, they allowed a competing system offering competing answers to the words of God. The therapeutic mindset has become as dangerous to the church as the Canaanites were to Israel.

To criticize the presence of psychology in the church these days is bordering on heresy. *What fellowship does light have with darkness* does not seem to be a question many believers are asking. Believers seem unaware that the therapeutic way devalues the Word of God and sidelines the Gospel of Jesus Christ. The degree to which psychology influences believers, is the degree to which believers do not see the necessity of the sufficient Word. Sanctification is stymied by disobedience. Bible memorization, reverence, worship and Christ-likeness fall to the wayside. Instead of mourning the demise of these virtues, we "celebrate recovery." After all, the way of the Word is slow. The ways of God are mysterious. The therapeutic way is tangible and the steps to healing are not as arduous and difficult as searching the Scriptures, prayer, faith and obedience.

God demands obedience. Psychology, on "scientific" grounds, helps an individual justify disobedience using the

"I can't" excuse. This excuse covers every conceivable sin. "I can't trust God because my earthly father left my mother and me when I was six years old; I can't control my tongue because I have an outspoken disposition; I am critical of the way my wife does things because I am a perfectionist; I can't because… I am strong-willed; I can't because… I was hurt in the past." Psychology provides people with scientific-sounding terms like addiction, compulsion, syndrome, disorder, chemical imbalance and disease. It comes to our rescue with all sorts of ways to justify our unbelief and disobedience.

Christians, who have prided themselves on their adherence to the inerrant Word of God, have lost confidence in the Word. They have placed their greatest dependence upon therapeutic answers for "real" issues of life. I grew up as a Southern Baptist where the supremacy of Scripture was believed and taught. The supremacy is still proclaimed among conservative believers everywhere; however, the relevance of God's Word to every day problems has eroded with the acceptance of psychology. The fallacy of the silence of Scripture in speaking and addressing behaviors and moods, and the fallacy of the effectiveness of psychology are the reasons for this shift. Before an individual criticizes the role of the therapeutic mindset in the church, they better be ready to defend the Word of God against accusations that it is irrelevant when it comes to behaviors and moods.

A Shift from Theology to Psychology

When we look at God's Word and the psychological mindset we must ask ourselves: Can they exist together? Are they competitive? Does one undermine and subvert the other?

Language is the tool of both theologian and therapist. In the mid-1960s a shift occurred in the way Christians view sin and disease. The church, under the influence of the therapeutic way of viewing life and living, stopped calling sin sin and started referring to it as sickness. The sexual sinner Paul wrote about (1 Corinthians 6:9) became the sex addict. The thief (1 Corinthians 6:10) became the kleptomaniac. The drunkard (1 Corinthians 6:10) became the alcoholic. The rebellious child (2 Timothy 3:2) became afflicted with "Oppositional Defiant Disorder." The liar is called a pathological liar. The gambler is a compulsive gambler. The idolater became a person who suffers from an obsessive compulsive disorder. The church has lost sight of the fact that sin is the root of many problems and the source of many people's troubles and moods. Biblical definitions and categories have changed and a new vocabulary related to disorders, "isms", and chemical imbalances has emerged within the church.

Has this dramatic shift in language provided us with a truer, more scientific understanding of people and their problems? Do these updated definitions of observable behaviors and moods really better describe reality or destroy reality? The answer we give will determine whether we look to Jesus Christ or a therapist.

The way we view *self* has changed as a result of the influence of psychology. From our biblical background "self" words such as self-control, self-denial and self-surrender, have been changed into therapeutically correct words like self-actualization, self-realization, self-fulfillment and self-awareness. The biblical self-hyphenated words relate to the character of God and how we are to be like Him. Character, a means of defining self, spoke of righteousness, integrity and right action. The man was an honest and kind man. The woman was a generous and virtuous woman. Character was formed as a person held to certain convictions and lived up to those convictions. In contrast, the therapeutic words focus on personality. This change from character, **"be ye holy for I am holy,"** (1 Peter 1:5) to personality required no value judgment, which was the goal of the psychological way. Personality was no longer based on convictions, moral expectations and godliness. Instead its focus was the individual's freedom of expression, fulfillment and gratification.

The psychological mindset has taken the words of God by which we previously have measured ourselves, words like patience, kindness, humility, meekness, and substituted self words, whereby we measure ourselves by ourselves, words like self-affirmation, self-confidence, self-conscious and self-interest. We have taken the God words and exiled them with God, replacing them with our own words which we prefer. We have looked inwardly, psychologized our lives and "freed" ourselves from the old ways. It feels so much better. Our hearts approve.

When we bring psychology into the church, we lay claim to another area of our lives which God once occupied. We seek therapy for the same reasons we once sought God. We hurt. We are sick. Depression has overwhelmed us and we feel we cannot go on. The same struggles that once motivated us to seek the face of God point us in another direction. If the axe had been laid at the root of the therapeutic tree years ago, as a minority of Christian leaders advocated, the church may have been spared a great many errors. Unfortunately, to appease them, the top of the tree was lopped off and has since sent out new branches with thicker foliage.

The teachings of Christianity that provided the overall framework for our society have been slowly eroding away. We have been methodically secularized. This has made the way for the psychological mindset. The changes came gradually. Minute changes generally go unnoticed. Whereas God was once the reference point by which we oriented our lives, now it is the pursuit of happiness, self-fulfillment and self-esteem. Now life is about solving a series of self problems instead of knowing Jesus Christ. Life is viewed in terms of systems, categories and diagnoses. We have embraced the therapeutic way and are more than willing to be analyzed and labeled by it.

It gives us a sense, even for awhile, that life is understandable and controllable. We can understand ourselves and others. When discussing a puzzling or odd individual, one only has to use a psychological label to help everyone understand. "He is bipolar." The conversation is over. The individual is summed up and reduced by a psychological label.

Psychiatrist Robert Cole, in his book, _The Secular Mind_, wrote, "With God gone for so many intellectual pioneers of the last two centuries, the rest of us, as students and readers, as seekers mightily under their influence, have only ourselves left as 'objects' of attention."[46] We have allowed our attention to shift from theology to philosophy. Psychology has reduced us to animals. We are no longer spiritual and material beings, we are just material. We look to neuroanatomy and neurochemistry for clues to who we are and why we do what we do. Our lives are defined in terms of biology, genetics, chemistry and brain function. We lose our awareness of how problems of living are connected to fellowship with God. Our humanity is reduced, and like the Israelites who accommodated the ideas of the Canaanites, we lose sight of the glory for which we are meant to live and aspire.

46 Robert Cole, _The Secular Mind_, (Princeton, NJ: Princeton University Press, 1999), p. 123

Chapter Five
Lessons from the Reformation

Remember those who led you, who spoke the
word of God to you; and considering the result of
their conduct, imitate their faith. Jesus Christ *is*
the same yesterday and today and forever.
Hebrews 13:7, 8

Woe to you, scribes and Pharisees, hypocrites!
For you build the tombs of the prophets and
adorn the monuments of the righteous, and say,
"If we had been *living* in the days of our fathers,
we would not have been partners with them
in *shedding* the blood of the prophets." "So you
testify against yourselves, that you are sons of
those who murdered the prophets. Fill up, then,
the measure *of the guilt* of your fathers.
Matthew 23:29-32

The question our forefathers frequently asked was, "how
are things going with the church?" The condition of the church
was the most important thing to them. It was not because they
were separatists and retreated from the world. Their concern
was motivated by the conviction that the state of the church
determined and regulated the state of society. Many still
believe this to be true today. What sets believers apart from
unbelievers is that believers view everything from the standpoint
of God's Holy Word. We look to Scripture for an explanation
of everything. Most people look to political, economical, and
educational sources for societal problems. However, with the
rise of the therapeutic mindset, psychological explanations have
been a major focus.

I think looking back to the Protestant Reformation would be useful in helping us better understand our present situation as it pertains to psychology. Some insist that going back is not useful. They especially do not see how going back five hundred years and reexamining the Reformation would be helpful. They say we must not look backwards for the solution, but forward, and that the church must do what others in every other realm of life are doing. We must look at the present situation in light of today's knowledge and understanding of man. We must use modern methods, techniques and strategies. We should consult the behavioral experts. We must research the latest and most up-to-date theories and therapies. I insist this is exactly what we have been doing. More of the same psychology is not the answer; it is the problem.

Why, with all our understanding of the nature of man and his problems, should we consider events that happened 500 years ago? Psychologically speaking, it is like going back to the horse or oxcart. How does the Reformation have meaning and instruction for us today? The answer is that it provides not just one of many possible explanations for the terrible state of the church and society, but *the* explanation and the way out. Ecclesiastical leaders compromised the Word of God. They integrated Scripture with all kinds of mystery religions, myths and secular ideas just like today. Prior to the Reformation the church, like today, was producing people who were almost totally ignorant of God's Word. As pertaining to ungodliness and unrighteousness, there was then and still are today, vice, immorality and rampant sin. At the same time, there was a denial of sin. And while sin was referred to as sickness back in the days of the Reformation, it was more commonly used in a metaphorical sense. In our day however, we have dropped the metaphorical use and think of sin as sickness in a literal sense.

What about the authority of the church? What about doctrine? Prior to the Reformation there was confusion over the church and doctrine. Is there anything more characteristic of the church today than doctrinal confusion and indifference? Many view doctrine as being divisive. Look at the ecumenical spirit we see growing today. The ecumenicalism of our time is not just the integration of Protestantism, Catholicism and so on, but the psychological way has been Christianized and made a part of the church's religious teachings.

I believe our focus on the present has not only complicated problems in the church and in society, but is, to a large extent, part of the problem itself. I believe we can find significant examples in Scripture admonishing believers to look back rather than look to the present.

If you recall, the children of Israel, like us, were very prone to unbelief. They believed it was better to look to the present than to look back. In contrast, God always called them to look back and remember the past. **"You shall remember that you were a slave in the land of Egypt, and the LORD your God redeemed you"** (Deuteronomy 15:15). Great care was taken that the Israelites would not forget their redemption from Egypt. They were admonished time and time again to look back to that great event. God memorialized the event by making the month they were delivered the start of the New Year. **"This month shall be the beginning of months for you; it is to be the first month of the year to you"** (Exodus 12:2). A special command was given to, **"Observe the month of Abib and celebrate the Passover to the LORD your God, for in the month of Abib the LORD your God brought you out of Egypt by night"** (Deuteronomy 16:1). Their deliverance was commemorated by the observance of the Passover. **"Now this day will be a memorial to you, and you shall celebrate it *as* a feast to the LORD; throughout your generations you are to celebrate it *as* a permanent ordinance"** (Exodus 12:14). The first of the Ten Commandments encourages them to look back to their deliverance. **"I am the LORD your God, who brought you out of the land of Egypt, out of the**

house of slavery" (Exodus 20:2). Time and time again the Israelites were instructed to look back.

Jesus commanded the church to look back when He instituted the Lord's Supper. What is the Lord's Supper? It is a memorial. It is believers gathering around the table and looking back. See how the unleavened bread has been broken into pieces. It is there to remind us of His broken body. The juice is a symbol of His blood that was shed for the remission of our sins. Jesus said, **"This is My body, which is for you; do this in remembrance of Me. This cup is the new covenant in My blood; do this, as often as you drink *it*, in remembrance of Me"** (1 Corinthians 11:24-25). Everywhere God's people are instructed as to the importance of looking backwards and remembering. Paul said, **"*Remember* that you were at that time separate from Christ, excluded from the commonwealth of Israel, and strangers to the covenants of promise, having no hope and without God in the world. But now in Christ Jesus you who formerly were far off have been brought near by the blood of Christ"** (Ephesians 2:12, 13, italics mine).

There is a right way and wrong way of looking at a great event like the Reformation. In Hebrews 13:7, 8 we have an example of how we should approach and examine the Reformation in light of our situation today. The writer admonished his readers to "remember" them. Remember the men who have spoken the Word of God in the past. We are told to consider **"the result of their conduct"** and **"imitate their faith"**. The Reformers remembered what had been written. They imitated Christ, the prophets, apostles and godly men and women before them. We need to look back at them. Modern theories and techniques do not nullify God's Word because **"Jesus Christ *is* the same yesterday and today and forever."**

Look Back: The Bible

Everyone is aware that the contemporary church has grown weak. Church leaders are trying to detect the cause. They have their theories and solutions. Many are rejoicing because the church and psychology are drawing nearer together. They talk about the "insights" drawn from the teachings of William James and dozens of others. The present, they say, is no time to discount the "contributions" of these men. Christians are hurting.

The devil's wiles will always zero in on drawing believers away from the sufficiency of Scripture. In Luther's day as in ours, there was no confidence in the Bible, no confidence that Scripture, without outside aid could provide answers to salvation and sanctification. Church leaders would assist parishioners in understanding the Bible. In the same way, psychology is believed to be a necessary supplement to the Bible and helps us to understand the nature of man, his problems and solutions.

The parallel between then and now is not exact, but it is close. While the inerrancy and sufficiency of Scripture is enthusiastically endorsed by most believers, there is not much confidence that the Word of God can accomplish its sanctifying purpose apart from psychology. Scripture is believed to be insufficient for the nurture and growth of believers specifically and the church in general. To make the Bible more effective we do not turn to the decrees of ecclesiastical leaders. Our trust, as evangelical believers, is in the modern enterprise of psychology. Through it we think mighty things will happen. However, in both the time of the Reformation and the psychologized church of today, *unbelief* is at work.

The men of the Reformation were men who believed in the authority of Scripture. They believed the Bible alone was sufficient for life and godliness (2 Peter 1:3). They faithfully and unapologetically "spoke the word of God" in a time of ecclesiastical and secular immorality and corruption. The pre-Reformation church, like the church today, was a church in decline, slumbering under the umbrella of biblical ignorance and unbelief. It was drowning in its own fluid of compromise. Like the Israelites who tolerated the ways and beliefs of the Canaanites, the pre-Reformation church and the church today are filled with strange doctrines, myths and speculations (1 Timothy 1:3, 4). What could be stranger than the gods, rituals and rites of the Canaanites which were eventually integrated into the Israelites' worship of Jehovah? What could be stranger than Freud's id, ego and superego or Eric Fromm's "common core" which the church has integrated into its theology of man? The wickedness of compromise was and is the slippery slope that has led to such deplorable partnerships common then and now.

Compromise turns convictions topsy-turvy. God's complaint against Ephraim is applicable to both the pre-Reformation church and the church today. God said through the prophet Hosea, **"I have written to him the great things of my law, but they were counted as a strange thing"** (8:12, KJV). What God has written is **"counted as a strange thing!"** The bizarre philosophies of men are no longer astonishing, but God's words are peculiar and odd. Man's foolishness is wisdom and God's wisdom is foolishness. Compromising God's Holy Word, then and now, has led to confused and disordered thinking.

The greatest leap of blind faith is when Christians entrust their lives to the "experts" in the fields of psychology and psychiatry. The psychological mindset with its hundreds of theories and therapies is presented to us as though it is verifiable truth. Its observations are touted as being "hard" knowledge, its beliefs grounded in "science," and its prejudices presented as facts. The result is that many believers accept the idea that the secularized concepts that pertain to their particular field or occupation really do constitute neutral knowledge and thus require no biblical critique. Their Christian faith is seen as an add-on to their private life.

The secular way offers people a "scientific" explanation of life rather than a life of faith in God's Holy Word. Thomas Szasz, in his book, *The Myth of Mental Illness*, wrote, "Mental illness is a myth. Psychiatrists are not concerned with mental illnesses and their treatments. In actual practice they deal with personal, social, and ethical problems of living."[47] Psychology helps us to deny and explain away personal, social, and moral problems by labeling them as psychiatric disorders. When Szasz traced the historical development of the idea of mental illness, he concluded it was not a science. Szasz said that linking mental illness with science and medicine was a way to free it from its long time association with quackery.[48] Medical language is used to gain the credibility and respectability of science and apply it to the problems and issues of life.

Consider believers who practice integration of Scripture with psychology. Although they would never agree with the atheistic foundations and presuppositions inherent in psychology, they do believe that psychology, being a "science," must be limited to materialistic causes. Unbelievers and believers alike can therefore pursue answers to psychological issues without evoking God. Our views of behavior and moods are methodologically atheistic. We have allowed atheists to define science and man. The church, having put a Christian spin to psychology, is for the most part satisfied. However, its mixture of theology and psychology reduces theology to subjective gloss. If man and his problems can be explained without evoking God, then laying psychology over theology as Christian counselors do is meaningless and unnecessary.

---

47 Thomas Szasz, *The Myth of Mental Illness*, (New York: Harper & Row Publishers, 1974), p. 262.
48 *Ibid* p., 182.

It is sad that many sincere believers keep stumbling over the same therapeutic step. They embrace biblical doctrine with their minds, follow biblical ethics in their practical behavior, but they still conduct their counseling on the basis of a materialistic worldview. You might say that "Room A" is where they confess their Christian beliefs, but in their pursuit of a counseling model they must move to "Room B." By contrast the sufficiency of Scripture for all matters pertaining to life and godliness does not require moving from one worldview to the other. True Science, not the pseudo-science of psychology, glorifies the Creator. Science takes Christianity out of the material versus immaterial rooms and places it in one big room. Christianity is restored to its proper status as genuine knowledge.

Biblical truth is often viewed by the world as foolishness. Paul spoke about the conflict between human philosophy and biblical truth when he said, **"The foolishness of God is wiser than men, and the weakness of God is stronger than men"** (1 Corinthians 1:25). God's wisdom may not appear, under the scrutiny of man, to be wise. In a pragmatic age like ours, what is true may be contrary to what works, or what is right may be different from what is acceptable. However, this does not mean there is a deficiency in God's Word, but it underscores the limitedness of human wisdom.

Like our society and the church today, the Greeks worshipped human wisdom. The word philosophy means "love of wisdom." New converts to Christianity at the church of Corinth wanted to hang on to their love of human wisdom. Human wisdom was believed to enhance divine revelation.

Paul's argument was not anti-intellectual and against natural facts or rational truth. Paul appealed to believers to think and understand when he said, **"And do not be conformed to this world, but be transformed by the renewing of your mind"** (Romans 12:2); and **"For this reason also, since the day we**

heard of it, we have not ceased to pray for you and to ask that you may be filled with the knowledge of His will in all spiritual wisdom and understanding" (Colossians 1:9). To know truth requires diligent study. Truth is understood rationally and not by a mystical impulse, feeling, or intuition.

Look Back: Who We Are

Christianity and psychology both claim to help us answer the question, "Who are we?" They give diametrically opposed answers. Christianity teaches we are not the same as the animals. We are made in the image and likeness of God. We are eternal beings. We are dependent upon the counsel of God's Word to understand the world and ourselves. The therapeutic way, in contrast, is about looking inward using our natural capabilities and creating a rational system to explain what we observe about ourselves. It is man's belief that he can accurately understand himself and the world around him without God.

The plethora of psychological theories about man and lack of consensus among them prove just how unsettled man is about who he is. To reject the spiritual side of man, by imposing competing secular explanations, will never explain that "something more" we have in our hearts. God fashioned man out of the dust of the earth, but then God breathed His own breath into him and made man a living being. One side of man is visible, the other invisible, one tangible and the other intangible. Man is a blend of mortal and immortal. We will never know who we are until we understand that man is a spiritual being living as an earthly being. When the church became enmeshed with psychology, man was reduced to the visible, tangible and mortal. We lost the vision of godliness and Christ-likeness; instead we adjust to the flesh and the world.

The opposing ideas inherent in psychology make the church's eager reception of it surprisingly strange. Nevertheless, because we are flesh and spirit, we will never be reduced to biology or chemistry. We are divided beings. The Old and New Testament believers all lived in constant awareness of the division within their nature. They spoke of two realities; one earthly, the other heavenly. Jesus told Nicodemus he must be spiritually reborn if he is to see the kingdom of heaven. Nicodemus did not understand and thought Jesus was talking about returning to his mother's womb and being reborn physically. Jesus explained the difference when he said, **"That which is born of the flesh is flesh, and that which is born of the Spirit is spirit"** (John 3:6).

Who are we? The Bible tells us we are a complex blend of flesh and spirit. If we allow psychology to tell us who we are, defining us biologically, we will never understand our inner or outward struggles. Our awareness of living as spiritual and earthly beings will puzzle and worry us. We must look back to the sacred explanations to rediscover who we are.

Christianity	Psychology
We are dependent upon God to understand the world	Man can understand the world without God
We are made in the image of God	We are animals
Man is a blend of mortal and immortal	Man is mortal
Man is inherently sinful	Man is good
Man is an eternal being	Man is a temporal being
Godliness	Psychological wholeness
Conformity to Jesus Christ	Conformity to the world
Self-denial	Self-esteem
To know God and His Son	Self understanding

Look Back: Sin

In Luther's day, as in ours, people did not have a biblical understanding of the seriousness of sin. Luther sounded the alarm in opposition to what was widely believed. He said sin blinded and incapacitated man, crippling his ability to make his way back to God. Even the most excellent men, however endowed with righteousness and all virtues, are nonetheless ungodly and unrighteous, and merit God's wrath. Man is bankrupt and filled with self-righteousness.

Men are as much in the dark today as they were back then. Today there is a massive trivialization of sin and widespread glorification of self-righteousness. Offenses against God (ungodliness and unrighteousness) are reduced to bad feelings about self. Whereas biblical counsel addresses the issue of unrighteousness and righteousness – "you must not..." and "you must..." – psychology encourages the individual to be their own person, do their own thing, build their self-esteem and so on.

The outcome, says sociologist Philip Reiff, is "psychological man." Confessing sin is replaced by finding self. Reiff said, "Religious man was born to be saved, but psychological man was born to be pleased."[49] The preoccupation with self leaves no room for "unhealthy" thoughts of sin. "I believe" has been replaced with "I feel." "I have sinned" has been replaced with "I am somebody special." The loss of a sin framework has led to the biblical terms righteous and unrighteous being changed to the secular terms mature or immature, productive or unproductive, socially adjusted or maladjusted. The words describe the same behavior or action, but the new psychological designation makes them morally neutral. He is no longer angry, short-tempered and difficult to get along with, he is maladjusted. She is no longer a failure, she is an underachiever. The behavior was not sinful, it was inappropriate. Biblical language is filled

49 Rieff, *The Triumph of the Therapeutic*, 29

with moral implications; however, psychology has taught us not to think in moral categories. It is best for our mental health.

It is the purpose of the church and the therapist to help us articulate and understand what is wrong with us. The Bible tells us sin is the root of our problems and the source of many of our disturbing feelings, moods and behaviors. However, sin has fallen into disfavor today. Sin as sickness has gained such a foothold in our thinking that there is no longer much thought of personal sin. We give a token recognition in sermons and conversations to what used to be a strong and ominous word, but references to sin, for the most part, have disappeared along with the whole notion of offending God. Have we ceased sinning? No, we are just calling it something else. We are more sensitive and compassionate, therefore we use psychologically approved speech and language that is non-directive, non-judgmental and non-offensive. The church and society are turned into a walking collection of personality disorders and diseases. Sadly, they have been persuaded that the right medication is what they need to alleviate their pain. Using pseudo-scientific language they are reduced to a biological organism. The fullness and richness of their humanity, beings made in the image of God, is ignored.

Why do individuals perceive themselves increasingly in terms of disorders and diseases? I think the ultimate answer is that we have lost sight of God (ungodliness). Our reference point has vanished and a diagnosis is a way of explaining things and giving people an identity. Psychological labels encapsulate the problem and give a person permission to live a therapeutically approved lifestyle. The new identity simplifies the complex. It explains why our relationships are falling apart and why we feel so terrible. We inherit allies consisting of likeminded sufferers. They are our new community. They are our support. However, all this is not without a price. We must stop and ask ourselves: what is it we lose if we avoid sin by calling it sickness?

First, we lose our sense of responsibility. Instead of hard work, self-discipline and self-denial, which are valuable and necessary to sanctification, we take a passive role. We assume the role of a sick person although we are well. Doctor's appointments, medication and rest are prescribed. We are not expected to carry our load in the family. Stress aggravates our symptoms and therefore, we must take care of our self. Others will carry our load. We are burdened enough coping with the disease. We lose charge of our own lives. The experts are in charge.

Second, the challenges of life necessary to spiritual growth and maturity are lost. Character is formed out of hard work and struggles. Paul wrote, **"Discipline yourself for the purpose of godliness"** (1 Timothy 4:7). Godliness takes work. Is it any wonder the New Testament always describes the Christian life as a war, a race or a wrestling match? Putting off sin and putting on righteousness is not accomplished by sitting on the shady side of Christianity, but by striving and laboring (Colossians 1:29). Even our Lord learned obedience by the challenges He endured. Psychology tells us these struggles are not normal. We cannot change; therefore, we must learn to "cope." We avoid challenges. Learning to live with our addictions, disorders, obsessions and diseases is the best we can hope for. We develop our life around coping rather than changing and growing more like Jesus Christ.

Third, we have exchanged the sacred for the secularization of our views of life. The thinking of modern man has unquestionably been secularized. It would not be so bad had Christians held out against the drift toward secularism, but they did not. Psychology is one example of how the church handed over its intellectual authority and the seemingly effortless descent it made into secularism. Some of the most acclaimed thinkers in the church today are non-Christians, such as Abraham Maslow and Carl Jung. We read their books and cherish their ideas, but their ideas are not Christian. Why is there so little Christian thinking when it comes to man and his problems? Are there no sacred answers to moods and behaviors? Certainly there are answers. Then why does the church think psychologically and pragmatically, but not Christianly? Among believers today you will find views of man wholly determined by psychology. The loyalty of the average church goer to psychology is, in a practical sense, greater than their loyalty to Scripture.

Sacred explanations of man and his problems are trivialized by non-Christians and Christians alike. We meet together as worshiping beings, but life's difficulties are complicated and thus we must step out of our theological skins to analyze them. We believe we cannot think Christianly about depression, bipolar disorder and so on. The attitude has emptied the Christian life of its content and we have a that is unwilling to accept the consequences and biblical explanations for its decline. We have chosen the way of compromise. When we talk about troubles, common to us all, we default to a secular frame of reference. We use secular language. We use secular categories. Sacred words are no longer relevant. Our Christian vocabulary does not effectively describe the complexities of contemporary man.

The church's slavish devotion to psychology has led to many additions to and subtractions from the language of faith. The argument is that, since science has provided us with new insights into human nature, the old words simply do not work anymore. Words like damnation, repentance and sin, when spoken out loud, sound dreadfully archaic. They are words from an earlier time. They are words associated with guilt and punishment. They are words that judge us and leave us feeling uncomfortable, anxious or depressed. They are not helpful.

However, discarding the language of sin weakens and softens the full impact of the gospel. The grace of God is cherished most by those who realize their sinfulness most. When one realizes that he has sinned the stakes go up dramatically. Sinning sounds much more serious than saying "I have a made a mistake, a poor choice or I have an obsessive compulsive disorder." Paul wrote, **"For one will hardly die for a righteous man; though perhaps for the good man someone would dare even to die. But God demonstrates His own love toward us, in that while we were yet sinners, Christ died for us"** (Romans 5:7-8).

Sin matters. Grace and forgiveness can only be adequately experienced and understood when man's wickedness and sin is understood. The goodness and mercy of the prodigal son's father can not be understood apart from the son's rebellion and rejection of the father. It is a story of sin and grace. It is not just a story of a merciful and good father. It is also about a rebellious son. Peter wrote in his first Epistle, **"But you are a chosen people, a royal priesthood, a holy nation, a people belonging to God, that you may declare the praises of him who called you out of darkness into his wonderful light"** (2:9). The wonderful light can only be comprehended when one knows darkness. Therefore darkness is our only hope of knowing light. Sin is our only hope of knowing life-giving grace. Men will not know their need for grace and mercy apart from knowing their sin. The crucifixion, the crowning act of mankind's wickedness, was God the Father's crowning example of grace. It was sin's most infamous moment and grace's most supreme moment! In man's most wicked deed we see God's most gracious act.

Today the language of sin is said to be depressing and counter-productive to one's mental well-being. Man, by nature, wants something to cheer him up. The price we pay is genuine grace. Grace requires a vocabulary of sin. However, to admit to sin is to confess that something is wrong with *you*. It implies willful rebellion against God. It evokes feelings of responsibility, guilt and judgment.

Look Back: The Cross

Unlike the false teachers who gloried and boasted in the flesh, Paul said, **"But God forbid that I should glory, save in the cross of our Lord Jesus Christ, by whom the world is crucified unto me, and I unto the world"** (Galatians 6:14, KJV). This verse follows on what Paul previously said, **"As many as desire to make a fair show in the flesh, they constrain you to be circumcised; only lest they should suffer persecution for the cross of Christ"** (vv. 12-13). The false teachers in Paul's day, like today, were integrating ideas contrary to the teachings of the apostles. They taught that it was right to believe the gospel, but added the necessity of going back under the Jewish law and submitting to circumcision. These contradictory voices were going out in the name of the Christian church. All these teachers professed themselves to be believers and their teachings to be Christian. However, what they said was diametrically opposed to what Paul taught.

People usually glory in something. Many people, no matter how vile or debased their actions may be, glory in their shame. Some glory in their gifts, which are talents entrusted to them by God. Others glory in their wealth and prosperity. The Apostle Paul had many things in which he could have gloried. Paul said, **"Though I might also have confidence in the flesh. If any other man thinketh that he hath whereof he might trust in the flesh, I more: Circumcised the eighth day, of the stock of Israel, *of* the tribe of Benjamin, an Hebrew of the Hebrews; as touching the law, a Pharisee; Concerning zeal, persecuting the church; touching the righteousness which is in the law, blameless. But what things were gain to me, those I counted loss for Christ"** (Philippians 3:4-6, KJV). When Paul was saved he forsook all glorying in his genealogy, his education, and his orthodoxy to rituals and righteousness. He cast them all aside, counting them loss compared to gaining Christ.

These days most people do not glory in the cross. They cannot endure the thought of an effectual purgation of sin by the death of the Son of God. Yet that is what the cross means. That is why Paul was so bold to preach it everywhere he traveled. The cross and its atonement for sin were plain matters of fact to Paul. Although he knew many would despise and hate him, Paul nevertheless refused to "improve" his message by integrating it with the latest philosophical theories in order to "reach" more people.

We have psychologized the preaching of the cross in our day. The message of the cross today is laden with psychological euphemisms. Sin is called sickness and is denied implicitly or explicitly. Recovery has replaced repentance. A therapeutic cross is preached, where feelings, happiness, self-esteem and psychological healing are celebrated. As for Paul, he declared the bare-naked, blood-stained and despised message of the cross and he gloried in it! Christ died for the ungodly. Everybody born of Adam has been born in sin. We are miserable sinners. Sin has brought misery into every person's life. Life is one trial after another. Life is full of disappointments. Life is a matter of man doing things he does not want to do and not doing things he knows he ought to do. Life is filled with moral problems, moral failure and difficulty. Life is a constant struggle, but the cross brings freedom from the power of sin.

Today, with all the "wisdom" of the psychologies we are still in the same condition. Men have formulated theories, planned schemes, passed their acts of congress and we are none the better. There is no question that mankind has made remarkable progress, but do these improvements prove that man is better than he was 100, 500, 1000 or more years ago? Is there less anger, jealousy, hatred, or adultery in the human heart? Is there less divorce, war or murder?

After the Second World War, civilization boasted how that was the war to end all wars. Mankind beat his swords into ploughshares, but then molded them into nuclear missiles. Because there was no psychology in the days of the prophets and apostles it is believed that today we are more advanced humans. Is this true? We read how they were tempted, weak and eventually fell into sin. What sin? The very same sin that is rampant among us today. Our everyday experiences contradict the whole notion of the gradual and progressive development of mankind that is so firmly rooted in our psychologized culture and church. Man is no different than he ever was; and although he is more educated and knowledgeable, he is not more righteous. However, psychology has convinced man that he is not a spiritual and moral creature, but a materialistic creature not unlike a cockroach, rat or horse. His problem is that he needs more education and further enlightenment. Mankind is evolving into a higher type. Jesus Christ becomes a benevolent reformer of man's psyche.

So what is the true message? What is the true gospel? Paul answers the question with this glorious statement. **"God forbid that I should glory save in the cross of our Lord Jesus Christ"** (Galatians 6:14, KJV)." It was unthinkable to Paul that he should glory in anything other than Jesus Christ and His cross. The reason is that it is by Jesus' crucifixion we are saved. It is the cross of Jesus Christ that sets us free and gives us eternal life. The death of our Lord was not an accident or the greatest tragedy of all times. The crucifixion of Christ was not something regrettable, but something that excited Paul and caused him to rejoice and give thanks.

In Luther's day, as in ours, the belief in the sufficiency in Christ's death on the cross had been lost. Once again, the similarities then and now are not exact, but are close. What is similar is the idea that Christ's sacrifice on the cross for sin is offensive. While the Apostle Paul said he gloried in the cross and to glory in anything else would be unthinkable, it was foolishness and a stumbling block to everyone else. Even in the church today there is a growing belief that there are many paths to God. Furthermore, with the growing influence of psychology, resulting in the erosion of the concept of sin (calling sin sickness), the cross of Christ is seen more and more as being unnecessary. Believers once aspired after godliness and righteousness. Now they seek psychological wholeness.

Look Back: The Devil

The world in which we live is a battleground. The Apostle Paul exhorted the believers at Ephesus not to forget the *nature* of the battle. He gave them specific instructions on how to prepare themselves in order to successfully engage the enemy and obtain victory. Paul said, **"Be strong in the Lord, and in the power of his might. Put on the whole armor of God"** (Ephesians 6:10, KJV). He tells them why Christians need to prepare themselves. Paul said, **"For we wrestle not against flesh and blood, but against principalities, against powers, against the rulers of the darkness of this world, against spiritual wickedness in high *places*"** (v.12). There is nothing more urgent at the present time than for us to lay hold and remind ourselves of what Paul said about this mighty battle. His words provide us with the only true explanation for the state of society and the world in general. Paul's teaching is vital to our understanding of the difficulties, hardships and disturbing moods that upset and discourage us. It is absolutely essential to our understanding the biblical doctrine of progressive sanctification, in other words, becoming more like Jesus Christ.

First, Paul said, **"We wrestle"** (v.12). Paul is anxious for his readers to grasp the *intimate* nature of the problem. Wrestling is a contact sport. A wrestler will grab hold of his opponent and perform a maneuver to trip him or put him in a hold like a headlock or a bear hug. Next, Paul clarifies who we are *not* wrestling when he says, **"For we wrestle not against flesh and blood"** (v.12). Unfortunately, most people, with the rise of the therapeutic mindset, even in the church, believe we wrestle with flesh and blood. Paul's warning cannot be minimized. We must never believe it is just a case of two people who have disagreed, grown angry and are now estranged. It is not flesh and blood. It is not just the discomforting moods and unwanted feelings that life brings our way. To look at the problems from a materialistic point of view will fall extremely short of understanding them and finding a solution. There are unseen forces working in the background. Paul says our opponent is not flesh and blood, but we wrestle **"against principalities, against powers, against the rulers of the darkness of this world, against spiritual wickedness in high** *places.*" Paul is dealing with the underlying cause of problems everyone faces in life. There is nothing more urgent and realistic than to grasp this "something more" element.

To Christians, Paul's words are full of significance and encouragement. Paul said, **"By revelation there was made known to me the mystery"** (Ephesians 3:3). Paul did not say he had been studying and observing human behavior and problems and had come to some general conclusions as to how to approach and solve them. The Bible is God's book. It is God's revelation. We must always begin with God and not man. Paul, like all the authors of the Bible, wrote under the direction and influence of the Holy Spirit. **"For no prophecy was ever made by an act of human will, but men moved by the Holy Spirit spoke from God"** (2 Peter 1:21). The church is not one of a number of institutions that could provide needful help to individuals who are depressed or anxious. The church, through the prophets and apostles, is the recipient of God's Word. It is not more speculation and conjecture. The Bible is not helpful up to a certain point and then needing to be supplemented by man's wisdom. The message of the Bible is God's message and is designed to bring us back to Him.

The only way to understand human history is to realize that it is the result of "The Fall." The fall of humanity in the Garden of Eden is the key to understanding mankind's past, present, and future, as well as our own individual experiences. History is the story of a great conflict between God and the devil. The devil and his subsidiary powers have one goal, and that is to destroy the works of God. His main tactic is to produce chaos and confusion. His aim is to separate man from God. Satan aspires to prevent men and women from worshiping, obeying and living for the glory of God (which is ungodliness).

We must never let our guard down and forget the power of the devil. He is described as a "roaring lion" and "great dragon." The most preeminent of all Old and New Testament saints were tempted and succumbed to the tricks of the devil. The greatest example of Satan's power and confidence is found in the fact that he did not hesitate to attack Jesus Himself. Yes, Satan is alarmingly powerful, but his authority and power are limited. God is supremely powerful and His authority is unlimited. As he did in the life of Job, God allows the devil to exercise a certain amount of power in the world. It is all part of God's great purpose. It is a mystery, but in spite of the power and authority exercised by the devil in nature, animals and man, God sovereignly reigns and rules.

How does the devil exercise his power over man? The one characteristic of the devil that stands out above all others is his subtlety. He uses wiles, tricks, or schemes intended to ensnare or deceive. The main target of his attacks is man's mind. Unlike animals that act instinctively, man has the ability to think, reason, be logical and look at himself objectively. Although man is now in a fallen condition, in certain ways he is still a noble creature. The mind God has given him has the greatest natural capacity for power and ability and is unrivaled in all of creation. The devil concentrates his attacks on man's mind.

Paul made a general statement concerning this when he wrote, **"In which you formerly walked according to the course** of this world, according to the prince of the power of the air, of the spirit that is now working in the sons of disobedience" (Ephesians 2:2). It is a universal statement of all people. All mankind is influenced by "the course of this world," or the thinking, the outlook or mentality. By nature our minds are shaped and we are accustomed to a worldly mind and outlook. What is it that determines this worldly way of thinking? Paul said it is **"according to"** or determined and controlled by **"the prince of the power of the air, of the spirit that is now working in the sons of disobedience."** This worldly mindset is controlled by the devil himself.

The devil's activity is manifested in the way he *insinuates doubts* in the minds of men. He gradually introduces an idea in a subtle or indirect way. The serpent asked Eve, **"Indeed, has God said?"** Adam and Eve had never questioned the truthfulness of God before. The serpent came to Eve with his wily and stealthy question suggesting that God's words were untrustworthy. The most dramatic example is the situation described in Matthew 16. In Caesarea Philippi Peter made his famous confession. Jesus asked, **"Who do people say that the Son of Man is?"** Peter responded, **"You are the Christ, the Son of the living God."** Jesus praised Peter for his answer and said, **"flesh and blood did not reveal this to you, but my Father who is in heaven."** Jesus proceeded to tell of his upcoming arrest and crucifixion. Peter, taking Jesus aside, immediately objected and amazingly rebuked Him and said, **"God forbid it, Lord! This shall never happen to You."** Our Lord quickly condemned Peter for questioning His eternal mission, **"Get behind Me, Satan! You are a stumbling block to Me; for you are not setting your mind on God's interests, but man's."** Notice the contrast. The Father revealed to Peter who Jesus was. Satan was covertly behind Peter's thinking when Peter took Jesus aside and rebuked him saying, **"Get behind Me, Satan!"** It was the devil insinuating doubts in Peter's mind.

The devil's activity is also manifested in the way he *instigates false teachings* in the minds of men. Paul warned Timothy that in the last days **"some will fall away from the faith, paying attention to deceitful spirits and doctrines of demons"** (1 Timothy 4:1). The space given in the New Testament to the teachings about "doctrines of devils," "seducing spirits," "antichrists," "false prophets," and so on is amazing. All of this is the working of the devil to create doubt and confusion by instigating false teachings. These false teachers are in the church today.

The confusion in the church today is the work of the devil. All the boasting about modern knowledge is foolish. There is nothing new, for example, about the so-called Higher Criticism movement that denies the miracles, deity, and virgin birth of Jesus Christ. There is nothing original about the denial of sin. The apostles confronted and addressed these issues many times. "Has God said?" is changed to "God has not said." They said, "The Bible is inerrant," but now they say, "It is filled with errors" and cannot be trusted. Man, with his superior mind, can sift through the Bible and discern the truth from the errors. The minds of men have the final say and are the arbiters of truth. They once confessed, "The Scriptures are sufficient," but psychology has helped them to realize the Bible's inadequacies, and now they say, "The Scriptures are insufficient."

The devil has been engaged in this kind of activity from the very beginning. It is not new. Satan still insinuates doubts and instigates false teachings within the church. For example, listen to what the church is saying about sin. Evangelicals believe fornication is a sin; however, they also believe it is a sickness. If it is sin why does the church sometimes call it sickness? If it is sickness why does the church sometimes refer to it as sin? When you listen to what the church is saying today about fornication, anger, rebellion, etc., it is very hard to know what they mean. This is the work of "seducing spirits." Here are God's people professing their belief that the Bible is authoritative while at the same time disagreeing over the issue of what is sin and what is sickness. The devil must be rejoicing at how easily Christians are seduced and persuaded of a lie.

There is nothing that is more significant in this psychologized age than the way it has elevated man's mind and ignored what the Bible teaches about the devil. A believer's sanctification is almost always characterized as psychological wholeness via therapy. Helping believers overcome their hurts, their uncomfortable feelings, moods, and thoughts, all the while building their self-esteem, is believed to be the key to spiritual growth.[50] The whole process of a believer's sanctification has become the application of psychological therapies and techniques such as building your self-esteem, filling your "love tank," meeting your needs, understanding your past, making peace with yourself, and so on. Believers are encouraged through "Christian" counseling to look to therapy and Christ, and all will be well.

The Bible's approach to sanctification always deals with sin as sin. There is no confusion. We are instructed to put on the armor of God, because our battle is not with "flesh and blood," but with the devil and his highly organized army of demons. However, this is ridiculed as being simplistic thinking. The problem is not sin, it is sickness. We must help people recover from their diseases. They are afflicted with chemical imbalances and they need medication to regulate the serotonin in their brain. They are suffering from compulsive thoughts or addictive behaviors which are diseases. These are all materialistic explanations. The problems are physical, like diabetes. We do not need to worry about the devil.

The way the devil attacks believers is found in the words **"scheme"** (Ephesians 6:11, NAS) or **"wiles"** (KJV). In Genesis 3

---

50 I have written on the subject of self-esteem sanctification in my books, *Jesus Christ: Self-Denial or Self-Esteem,* (Published by Timeless Texts), and *Self-Esteem; Are We Better Than We Think?* (Published by Personal Freedom Outreach).

we read "Now the serpent was more crafty than any beast of the field." Paul wrote, **"But I am afraid that, as the serpent deceived Eve by his craftiness, your minds will be led astray from the simplicity and purity** *of devotion* **to Christ"** (2 Corinthians 11:3). Paul warned us not to be ignorant of the devil's methods of tripping us up when he wrote, **"For to this end also I wrote… so that no** *advantage* **would be taken of us by Satan, for we are** *not ignorant of his schemes"* (2 Corinthians 2:9, 11, italics mine). The devil will do all he can to get an advantage over believers in order to bring disgrace upon God.

Another example of safeguarding Christians from the devil is when Paul speaks about ordaining a novice as pastor. Paul wrote, **"and not a new convert, so that he will not become conceited and fall into the condemnation incurred by the devil. And he must have a good reputation with those outside** *the church,* **so that he will not fall into reproach and the** *snare* **of the devil"** (1 Timothy 3:6-7, italics mine). The art of setting a trap to catch a rabbit or bird is to conceal it with sticks and leaves. Traps are not placed in open areas, but in wooded and grassy places. The trap is most effective when it blends in with its surroundings. The animal does not see the snare, but is attracted by the bait. Subtlety is the key to trapping animals *and* people.

The devil uses lies as part of his wiles or schemes. Jesus said that when the devil, **"speaks a lie, he speaks from his own** *nature,* **for he is a liar and the father of lies"** (John 8:44). The popular belief among believers that the concepts of psychology are not dangerous is a lie. The devil does not speak the truth about anything. He is always ready to twist the truth as a method of causing confusion. The devil tempted Adam and Eve with a lie. He calls evil good and good evil. His words are intended to trap us and mislead us away from God. Lying is the language peculiar to Satan. It is his style, his form of expression and his characteristic way of speaking. When men lie they borrow it from the devil. It is the devil who has filled their heart with untruthfulness (Acts 5:3). He is not just the father of his own lies, but the lies of others. He is the father of every lie.

Paul sarcastically condemned the believers at Corinth because they had repeatedly listened to and were misled by false teachers. He said, **"For if one comes and preaches another Jesus whom we have not preached, or you receive a different spirit which you have not received, or a different gospel which you have not accepted,** *you bear this beautifully"* (2 Corinthians 11:4, italics mine). Paul wonders at their naiveté and poor judgment. These believers were always ready to listen to corrupt men and be taken captive by their plausible yet specious ideas. The believers at Corinth were ignorant of "the wiles of the devil."

Again Paul said, **"As a result, we are no longer to be children, tossed here and there by waves and carried about by every wind of doctrine, by the trickery of men, by craftiness in deceitful scheming."** (Ephesians 4:14). Paul warns us against seducers. We must take care that we are not like children who are weak in faith and knowledge, easily yielding to the mischievous subtlety of false teachers.

Paul told Timothy to be prepared because in the "later times," which we are in right now, there will be a movement away from Christ and his teachings. **"But the Spirit explicitly says that in later times some will fall away from the faith, paying attention to deceitful spirits and doctrines of demons..."** (1 Timothy 4:1). The origin of this apostasy from Christ and His teachings is the devil and his army of "seducing spirits." They are demons whose object is to lead men away from Christ and bring confusion and chaos into the church. The tools they employ are men who themselves are unaware they are teaching the doctrines of demons.

How can we become aware of the schemes and wiles of the devil? How does the devil use them to deceive us? The key to understanding the way Satan works is found in 2 Corinthians 11:13. Paul said, **"For such men are false apostles, deceitful workers,** *disguising* **(NAS), or** *transforming* **(KJV) themselves as apostles of Christ** (parenthetical comment and adaptation mine). It is not surprising that false teachers disguise themselves. Paul said, **"No wonder, for even Satan disguises himself as an angel of light"** (v. 14). Satan transforms or changes himself into something he is not, an angel of light. The devil puts on a mask as it were. He becomes an actor who plays different characters which makes him and his works more difficult to detect. When Satan came to Eve the Bible said he "beguiled" and deceived her. He did not come as a roaring lion. A roaring lion is not very subtle. He takes off the lion mask and puts on another more pleasing and enticing mask. He comes as a friend who wants to help you. Recall his words to Eve, **"Indeed, has God said?"** The devil comes at times as someone who is looking out for our well-being, enticing us away from God and His Word.

Another method the devil uses is *insinuation*. He comes to us and does not say anything directly; instead, he suggests or insinuates something. For example, the devil said to Jesus in the wilderness, **"If you are the Son of God…"** (Luke 4:3). He did not say Jesus wasn't the Son of God, but he implied it using innuendo. Using the same tactic he may come to you and ask "Is not all truth God's truth?" or "The Bible speaks sufficiently with regards to salvation, but does it speak sufficiently to sanctification? Could not psychology benefit and enhance what the Bible says with regards to man and his problems?" And so the devil comes to us as a friend who wants to enlighten us in the Scriptures.

Another of Satan's strategies, or masks, is probably the cleverest of all. The devil hides himself altogether and propagates the idea that there is no devil. The devil is not our problem today. The idea that the devil is behind "addictions or compulsions" is considered ludicrous. Psychology has proven the sin of drunkenness is really the disease of alcoholism; the sin of anger is the disease of anger addiction; the sin of rebellion is the disease of oppositional defiant disorder, and so on. Most Christians do not deny the fact of the devil and his seducing spirits; they just deny him with regards to sinful behavior relabeled as disease. They believe it is absurd to think the problem is spiritual in nature. They do not believe they are "wrestling with flesh and blood" and "principalities and powers."

The devil is at his best when he persuades people he does not exist, or he is not actively involved in the circumstances of their lives. With regards to the psychological mindset, the church has denied the activity of the devil. The church is drugged and deluded. The church is asleep. The church is not aware of the conflict in which it is immersed. The church is not alarmed.

The devil has instigated movements and spread myths and speculations that have resulted in the belief in doctrines of demons. This belief has affected the lives of Christians. There have been all sorts of movements initiated by the devil that have become part of the thinking of Christian people.

The psychological mindset ridicules this teaching. The fatal mistake lies in believing that man is a material being only and does not have a spiritual side. Man's problems are explained in terms of a conglomeration of diseases, disorders and chemical imbalances. This is the basis of the entire secular teaching and the psychological way of viewing man. Do not forget Paul is addressing the ultimate cause of problems. He puts it into the context of a battle that is difficult and strenuous. He reminds us he is not expressing his own opinions, but he is teaching us what he has received by revelation from God. Thus it is the only way to effectively deal with problems. Other explanations are inherently competitive. The attitude which says the Bible is deficient and psychology is a necessary and valuable appendage is a denial of everything the New Testament teaches about the sufficiency of Scripture and the sanctification of man.

Christian leaders and thinkers sometimes fail to differentiate between a cause and effect. A medical analogy may be useful. For example, part of the job of the physician is to correctly diagnose the problem, (so is the job of a psychologist or biblical counselor). The patient usually has a primary problem, for example, pneumonia. (The primary problem for the counselor may be anger, depression, rebelliousness...). The primary disease is in the patient's lungs. (The psychologist says the primary problem is chemical imbalance which cases the behavior and labels it ADHD. The biblical counselor says the primary problem is a sin/heart issue.) With pneumonia there will be a variety of symptoms such as fever, sweating, fatigue, general aches and pains. (In our analogy the symptoms are anger, depression, self-pity, rebellion...). The danger is spending time medicating symptoms and not attacking the disease. A person may take a pain reliever to alleviate his headache and muscle pain, but it will not have any effect on the pneumonia. It is the pneumonia, not the symptoms that matter.

Psychology deals with symptoms, i.e., the child is rebellious and won't pay attention, speaks out of turn, etc. The psychologist, as well as the biblical counselor, see the same behavior. It is the explanation of the behavior where we differ. In this example, the psychologist says it is ADHD. The biblical counselor says it is sin—the heart. The psychologist addresses the symptom. The biblical counselor addresses the disease.

The problem is that people do not understand the cause of tribulations and difficulties. They think the cause is human. The manifestations of troubles are symptoms. The cause is unseen and spiritual. That is what the world does not understand. The Christian Church alone has the message that identifies the cause and the remedy. The tragedy is that the church, much of the time, is saying the same thing that the world, and in particular psychology, is saying. Wanting to give the impression it is relevant, the church mimics the terminology of popular psychology. How pitiful! It would be laughable if it were not so tragic and sad. They are ignoring the disease and medicating symptoms.

"Wherefore take unto you the whole armor of God that ye may be able to withstand in the evil day, and having done all, to stand" Ephesians 6:13, KJV). The words armor, stand and withstand all depict the fierceness and the severity of the battle. You may repulse an attack, but you can be sure there will be another and another. The enemy is strong, and so we should be **"strong in the Lord and in the power of his might"** (v. 10, KJV), and persistent. Believers will experience many "evil days" throughout their journey in this life. We are involved in a relentless conflict, and our failure to understand it may result in our losing our balance, being thrown to the ground and knocked out. We must do all we can to "stand" and "withstand" the continuous assaults against us. It is important that these things are part of our thinking.

The church is fooling itself in the way it has compromised the Word of God and has bought into it psychology's explanation that the cause of man's problems is man himself. In other words, it is all materialistic. It is biology. It is brain chemistry. The spiritual element is rejected and ridiculed. The whole foundation of the psychological view rests on the assumption that we *are* wrestling with flesh and blood. The problem is man, and therefore the answer can be solved by man. The thoughts and theories of the natural man never rise any higher. It is always flesh and blood. The spiritual element is never considered.

The cause is not human. We wrestle not with flesh and blood, but **"against principalities, against powers, against the rulers of the darkness of this world, against spiritual wickedness in high *places*"** (Ephesians 6:12). Our troubles are not with other men, but ultimately, with the devil and his army of unseen forces. But the whole idea of believing in the devil is rejected and ridiculed. Believing in unseen spiritual forces, in an age of science, technology and advancements in psychology are considered irrational and superstitious. When people are hurting and struggling they need something practical. The explanation set forth by Paul would be an insult to modern man's intelligence. It is folklore, myth and legend and a manifestation of primitive thinking. What is disturbing is that believers are not emphasizing and giving attention to these spiritual matters. People, they insist, have bipolar disorder, ADHD, obsessive compulsive disorder, depression, chemical imbalances and so on. The problems are biological in nature and not spiritual.

The confusion in the church over the sufficiency of God's words is nothing new. The devil has been engaged in this activity since the beginning. "Has God said?" There is nothing that makes man more foolish and shameful than his pride of intellect, his boast in his capacity for knowledge, or his rational or intelligent thought. He spouts forth the latest and newest ideas that are in reality just the same old ideas, but in modern terminology. It is tragic how the devil blinds people from the very beginning by introducing doubt and false teachings and so creates confusion in the church. One believer believes the Bible is *sufficient* to help people solve problems of living. Sin is sin. Another believes the Bible is *insufficient* when it comes to solving problems of living and the church must gain clearer understanding through psychology. Sin is called sin, but it is sometimes called sickness. Is the church confused? How pathetic and tragic!

The Good News

The condition in which the church finds itself is a result of its departure from the Word of God. Yes, the times are evil, but the times have always been evil. Over the history of the church there have been movements initiated by the devil which have affected the lives of Christians. His purpose is to disrupt the life of the church and the propagation of the gospel. The New Testament Epistles were written to counteract these efforts of the devil. We are involved in such a movement today.

Christian psychologists are the new highly honored and infallible priesthood. They too reject *sola scriptura*! They respond "all truth is God's truth." Believers no longer search the Bible to test whether what is being taught is Scriptural and not the doctrines of demons. Christian psychologists claim there is more truth than that which is found in the Holy Bible. New "revelations" have been uncovered through godless and antichristian prophets of psychology. These revelations are being touted to be just as true as the Bible. Incredibly, many pastors and Christian leaders approve equality of these theories with God's Word. Jesus said, **"I am *the* truth"** (John 14:6). Jesus is the source of all truth. How can psychology be another source of God's truth? Jesus' words exclude all others from being a source of truth. Is it not incredible?

Jesus said, **"Thy word is truth"** (John 17:17). He does not merely state God's word is true, but it is *the* truth. Christian psychology's mistake is to claim "all truth is God's truth." When they refer to "God's truth" they are referring to facts of nature or science; however, that is not what Jesus was talking about. Jesus said *"The truth* **shall set you free."** Understanding and knowing the facts of science will not set a person free. Christian psychology has broadened Jesus' words and distorted His meaning. The truth Jesus spoke about now encompasses not just who He is, **"I am the truth,"** but theories and ideas concocted by atheists. It is a total rejection of *sola scriptura*.

The good news is that, although prior to the Reformation the authority and sufficiency of the Bible had been denied, the Reformation still happened. The Bible was put into the hands of the common people, the gospel recovered, the church reinvigorated, and society was affected in a profound way. If the church then can be restored so can the church today.

Chapter Six
Philosophy: The Enemy of the Church

See to it that no one takes you captive through philosophy and empty deception, according to the tradition of men, according to the elementary principles of the world, rather than according to Christ.

Apostle Paul, Colossians 2:8

The early Puritan Christians believed all of life was lived before God. All of life was God-related. Jesus said, **"You are the salt of the earth"** (Matthew 5:13). The Puritans held the conviction that the church had a preserving effect on society. Jesus said, **"You are the light of the world"** (Matthew 5:14). They were persuaded that the church had an enlightening effect on society. The Puritans were very concerned about the condition of the church because of its effect on society as a whole. Therefore, when considering the state of society they would ask the question: "How are things going with the Church?"

In the days of the Puritans, as in our day, people tended to believe that problems, personal and societal, had political, economical and educational causes. Bad politics, the economy, or lack of education are what cause problems; therefore, the solutions are political, economical and educational. The right legislation would solve the poverty problem. Improvements in the economy would solve the rise in crime. The answer to the drug, alcohol and smoking problem is awareness and education. The Puritans, however, believed there was only one explanation to the problems of poverty, crime, drugs and alcohol, and that was sin.

The question, "How are things going with the Church?" is an important one. It is not a hard question to answer. Statistics tell us church membership is declining. Prayer meetings, missionary groups and other church functions are poorly attended. Many churches have cancelled mid-week or Sunday evening services, or both. Some of the mega-churches are growing, but for the most part they are market-driven, short on doctrine and big on feeling-oriented programs.

Historically, the problems with the condition of Israel in the Old Testament and the church in the New Testament time can be traced to a departure from God's Word. The departure began for us in the mid-nineteenth century with a movement to replace revelation with man's philosophies. The greatest enemy of the church has always been philosophy. Revelation is what God says is true. Philosophy is what man says is true. Philosophy is man's explanation of the origin of the universe, life, behavior and so on. Philosophy is man theorizing. It is man saying, "I do not need God. I can know." It is man's belief that his own mind is sufficient to understand life and the world. The serpent said to Eve, "You will be like God." Just as God can subjectively know, Eve could subjectively know. Adam and Eve would not need the counsel of God. It is at this very point when man was persuaded that he could know, that the schemes of the devil were so deceptive and effective.

In Genesis chapter three Satan focused on Eve's thinking. He did not come to Eve and beat her into submission with a club. Satan's strategy is always directed toward our thinking process, intellect and understanding.

Paul said, **"But I am afraid that, as the serpent deceived Eve by his craftiness, your minds will be led astray from the simplicity and purity *of devotion* to Christ"** (2 Corinthians 11:3). The devil's focus is on turning our minds from the "simplicity" of Christ to that which is complex, difficult and convoluted.

What could be more complicated than all the different and contradictory theories (about 300) of psychology?

Paul wrote, **"O Timothy, guard what has been entrusted to you, avoiding worldly *and* empty chatter *and* the opposing arguments of what is *falsely called 'knowledge'"*** (1 Timothy 6:20-21, italics mine). Many believers are governed by philosophies "falsely called knowledge" or science. How can you scientifically prove Freud's theory of the id, ego and superego? You can dissect a cadaver and you will find a heart, spleen and a stomach, but you will never find an id, ego or superego. It is just Freud's theory about man. Freud was trying to explain man and his moods and behaviors without God. Just as evolution is a pseudo-science, psychology is a pseudo-science.

The Bible always begins with the presupposition that man is a sinner; therefore, he cannot arrive at complete knowledge on his own. Man must depend upon God's counsel to understand life and the world. **"Let no man deceive himself. If any man among you thinks that he is wise in this age, he must become foolish, so that he may become wise"** (1 Corinthians 3:18). Paul said if we are going to be wise we must confess our tendency to be a philosopher and the inclination to trust in our own mind and ability to understand.

Many believers have wholeheartedly accepted as truth extra-biblical statements and authorities. The relationship between the Bible and science is not complicated. As long as science deals with facts, we should accept it. Real science always glorifies the Creator. Psychiatry and psychology are theories in the same way evolution is a theory. When people talk about evolution they are not being scientific, they are speaking as philosophers. When men talk about psychiatry and the therapeutic way, they too are speaking as philosophers and not being scientific.

The Bible teaches that mankind is blinded by the god of this world and cannot know truth apart from revelation. We must never accept speculation when it comes to understanding the nature of man. We must get our knowledge from the Bible. All other explanations are competitive with Scripture.

Psychology began to take hold in the Christian Church in the mid-1960s. Integration was the key word. Believers were taught that Christian theology needed psychology; however, psychology needed Christian theology. Psychology would help us better understand ourselves. Theology would help us better interpret psychology. The one was necessary to the other. The church began to promote psychology, man's wisdom, as a means of enhancing ministry, advancing spiritual growth and maturity or sanctification. It was Christian psychologist Clyde Narramore who popularized the trichotomist theory of man based on the therapeutic ideology. Narramore said there is now a specialist for each part of us. For your body there is the medical doctor. For your spirit there is the pastor. For your soul or mind there is the therapist.

The church had failed to take to heart Paul's warning: **"Be ye not unequally yoked together with unbelievers: for what fellowship hath righteousness with unrighteousness? and what communion hath light with darkness?"** (2 Corinthians 6:14, KJV). Or Paul's other warning: **"Your boasting is not good. Do you not know that a little leaven leavens the whole lump** of dough?"(1 Corinthians 5:6). By the 1970s seminaries were going full steam ahead integrating Christian theology and psychology. By the late 1980s psychological concepts had inundated every aspect of the church. Psychological categories replaced Bible ones. The rebellious child is not sinful, but sick. He has oppositional defiant disorder. Therapists trained in one of the 300 models of psychology were considered the experts when it came to people and their problems. Springing up all across the country were Christian in-patient clinics.

They teach that the Bible is not enough for sanctification. Yes, it is **"a lamp to my feet and a light to my path"** (Psalm 119:105). What does that mean from a practical standpoint? Some have said we do not live in the same world as the Psalmist. The complexities of our time require deeper wisdom. The psalmist didn't understand alcoholism or obsessive compulsive disorder. Those who attempt to integrate theology and psychology are convinced there is a need for higher wisdom than Scripture offers. Bona fide "professionals" and experts are required to understand human nature. They help believers who are anxious, fearful or depressed by filling in the gaps left in the Bible. These people have failed to discern the inherent contradictions between psychology and theology and, in doing so, unintentionally deny Scripture. They interpret biblical categories into psychological ones, thinking they are making the Bible more effective in helping people

Therapeutic churches, to various degrees, are found in every denomination. In Deuteronomy 7:1-6, when the children of Israel moved into the land God had promised to their fathers, God instructed them to destroy the people, cattle and buildings of worship (altars and pillars). In spite of God's warnings the people did not obey. God knew people would be tempted to incorporate what they conquered into their own culture. Soon, Israel was no longer pure, but was polluted by the very cultures they conquered. The consequences were catastrophic and led to judgment. It is no less catastrophic to see what the leaven of psychology has done in the church today. We have polluted the Christian message with psychology's language, excuses, theories and therapies. We have catered to people's "itching ears" and have replaced God's wisdom with man's. Psychology is just another idolatrous philosophy.

How is the state of the church? It is impossible to understand the state of the church and society as a whole without taking into consideration the way they have been influenced by psychology.

Every aspect of our culture, including public schools, Christian schools, the legal system, politics, health care, and Christian teaching have the roots of psychology growing deep into their institutions. Very few things can match psychology's influence upon the church's beliefs and practices. This is due mainly to the fact that psychology's techniques and practices are considered by believers to be neutral and harmless.

Those who promote psychology, like all integrationists, cast doubt on God's sufficient Word. The therapeutic mindset questions, ignores, embellishes, distorts, and contradicts the plain teaching of Scripture. If psychology appears to be an ally, it is only because the church has lost its orientation. People who have been "taken captive by philosophy" are "blind guides." They teach others to fix their eyes not on Jesus, but on Sigmund Freud, Carl Rogers, and others. They lead believers to trust man's wisdom and doubt God's Word, which is the hallmark of secular humanism. The church has reaped what it has sown. Sin is called sickness; evangelism and sanctification have drastically been affected.

Chapter Seven
"By All Means, Let Us Bury It"

The novelist G.K. Chesterton said that when
a man turns his back on God, he doesn't just
believe in nothing, he believes in anything.

Vinoth Ramachandra, *Gods that Fail*

The devil is never so subtle and successful as when he
succeeds in persuading *unbelievers* he does not exist. Satan
is never more subtle than when he persuades *believers* he
is not active in their particular situation, circumstance or
ideology. While he is very active in the theories and practices
of psychology, Christians, for the most part, do not think he
is. People believe that the conglomerations, mixed mass and
collection of psychological theories, although not founded on
empirical evidence, are, nevertheless, grounded in "science."
They naively believe psychology and its subsequent therapies,
as they pertain to Christian theology, are benign and neutral.
They believe psychology can benefit all other disciplines from
educational theory and practice, law, politics, the penal system,
Christian theology and many more.

Heresies

Heresies have been used successfully down through the
years by the devil to produce chaos and confusion in the church.
A heresy is a denial of an established Christian doctrine. A
heresy is more limited in scope than apostasy. Apostasy is a
total renunciation, denial, or misrepresentation of Christian
doctrine which leads to a denial and abandonment of the
whole of Christian truth. To be guilty of heresy means a person
holds true to the main beliefs of the Christian faith, but goes
wrong with regard to some particular doctrine or doctrines, for

example, the sufficiency of Scripture, the denial of sin (explicitly or implicitly by calling it sickness), or by replacing the biblical doctrine of man with one of psychology's theories of man.

The New Testament clearly demonstrates how heresies had already begun to establish themselves in the early church. Almost all the Epistles mention some heretical philosophy and practice the enemy had sown. The devil's purpose was to disrupt, shake the confidence of believers, and upset the work of God. The Epistles were written, in some respects, to counteract these heretical ideas. When Paul wrote, **"Be not deceived: evil communications corrupt good manners"** (1 Corinthians 15:33, KJV), he was warning believers of the danger of unbiblical philosophies. These teachings are not benign and harmless. Believers cannot afford to be indifferent. Christians must remember they are involved in a spiritual battle. We are not, as psychology teaches, wrestling with flesh and blood, but with a spiritual enemy that is cunning and powerful.

Doctrine is vital. If a believer goes wrong in his doctrine, he will ultimately go wrong in other areas of his life. His thinking and behavior will be affected. For example, what happens when problems and difficulties come his way? He has been misled to believe that the Bible is insufficient. He must look to one of the hundreds of psychological theories and practices to understand his actions, feelings and moods. He goes to counseling and learns his immoral behavior that has complicated his marriage is an addiction, i.e., a sickness, or he is suffering from Bipolar Disorder or some other "mental illness."

The real trouble with such a believer is that he has succumbed to the wiles of the devil, and has denied certain doctrines of the Christian faith. He has fallen for Satan's lies and has believed in one, or a combination of, the over two hundred psychologies promoted in the church today—lies such as "the Bible is insufficient," "sin is sickness" and "the nature of man and his behavior is best understood by the teaching of atheistic fathers of psychology."

Nothing is more important and relevant to the Christian today than understanding the heretical nature of psychology, and especially "Christian" psychology. Unbelievers who adhere to the theories and practices of psychology understand psychology's incompatibility with Christian theology. Unfortunately, many believers do not, and therefore have created their own form of psychology and call it Christian.

If we believe the Bible is insufficient for life and godliness then we look to other "truths." Every false teaching or cult has a particular person and their extra-biblical "revelation" or discovered "truth." This is true of psychology too. Christian psychology is also characterized by its devotion to a particular person or persons. Among them are Sigmund Freud, Carl Jung, Alfred Adler, Carl Rogers and so on.

The Holy Spirit is the power in the Christian Church. The Holy Spirit will never honor anything but His own Word. The Holy Spirit gave us the Scriptures. He is the Author. The Bible is not a product of "flesh and blood." If individual believers and the church in general deviate from the Bible, then we do not have any right to expect the blessings of God. The Holy Spirit will honor His Word and nothing else.

The major problem in the church today is that we are not honoring God's inerrant and sufficient Word and He is not honoring us. Sadly, we are all aware of the decline and weakness in the church. The church is lacking in power and its leaders are trying to figure out why. They jump to one conclusion and then another, but it seems that no one can figure it out.

One of the main troubles, we are told, is how people today are suffering from a variety of personal and interpersonal problems. Today's hectic lifestyle is believed to cause stress and nervous conditions in people unlike anything their parents or grandparents are said to have experienced. With cell phones, internet, cable and satellite television, temptations are everywhere. Troubles and tribulations are getting people down and the church is affected in every way. The church must understand and minister to its members who are having interpersonal problems, uncomfortable moods and feelings. It must provide "support" and counseling for those whose behaviors, moods and feelings stem from diseases, disorders and chemical imbalances. Strong and vibrant congregations must have emotionally whole members. We rejoice because Christian theology has drawn closer and closer to the psychologies. Mental illness is our great common enemy and the "truths" promoted by psychology will provide the remedy needed. Our churches will be strengthened.

This is all carnal thinking! The Bible teaches that only one thing matters and that is truth. Jesus said He is truth. Believers are sanctified by truth. Jesus said His Word, as opposed to men's words, is truth. He will not honor so-called psychological truth. There is no such thing as a single discipline called *psychology*. There are just *psychologies* and a proliferation of conflicting theories and therapies. Nevertheless, Christians talk about the "insights" of psychology. Ecclesiastical leaders tell us it is no time to ignore the wisdom of these great thinkers about the psyche. The result would be that Christians, their families, and churches everywhere will suffer. What a tragic failure to understand the nature of the problem and the basic teachings about the wiles of the devil.

The therapeutic way is a normal part of our everyday life. We take it for granted. We crack jokes about it and criticize it, but, like the weather, it is an unquestioned part of our world. It plays an integral role in our culture in defining what it means to be human. Individuals are understood to be containers of a "mind" or a "self" that needs therapy instead of a carrier of the divine image that needs to be saved. It influences standards of normality, criminality, trends in education, concepts of health and illness, morals, everyday language, and so on. It consists of a plethora of complex theories and ideologies. There is no objective *psychology*, there are only subjective *psychologies*. There is no consensus about what is wrong with a client or how to deal with their problem. It is tenaciously believed to be a scientific practice; however, it is anything but standardized and empirical.

For the past four decades or more, with growing disbelief, we have all witnessed the evangelical church plunge into theological illiteracy. At the same time, we have accepted a frame of reference constructed by secular thinkers. Thinkers who, while they are sincerely concerned about the state of the world, make judgments that are not Christian judgments and adopt views that are unbiblical views. It is all done in a way that years ago believers would have rejected outright, but today, even in the face of denying the spiritual dimension, is accepted and has become part of the way we think about theology.

Moving from a world where God and truth were considered central (even in a public place) to a world where they are neither did not happen overnight. It came gradually over time. God began to disappear from public view as the impersonal forces of secular humanism unleashed their ideas on the world. It was Charles Darwin's publication in 1859 of *The Origin of Species* that set in motion a revolution in thinking. Decades afterward, the idea of a natural world with no place for God was accepted by most intellectuals. Every discipline—academic, government and the church—was eventually reshaped to reflect evolutionary concepts. This prepared the way for the integration of Freudian doctrine into the church's view of man.

Modern evolutionists view nature as one big machine independent of God. Because humans are part of this machine, the study of human behavior is turned into a biological science. Our behavior, following the laws of nature, is reduced to genetics and chemicals. Adultery, lying, drunkenness, violence, kindness and love are explained in terms of genetics or chemicals. The gap between human and non-human became narrower and narrower until it finally disappeared. Anthropologists and experimental psychologists declared the unique qualities once thought to be characteristic of humans to be true of other animals as well. Supposedly, we humans are like all other species and organisms. It is only the size of our brains that make us different. It is arrogant and untrue to think we are special.

Before the 1960s only theologically liberal Christians embraced the psychologies. Pastoral counseling, believers trained in the fundamentals of human nature by psychologists, psychiatrists and social workers, was virtually synonymous with liberalism. The liberal church became part of an expanding network to provide mental health services. Meanwhile, conservative churches ignored counseling and focused on evangelism. They did not have the intellectual or institutional means to help people with problems of living. Believers with unresolved problems of life either suffered in silence or secretly made their way into the mental health system.

In the 1960s, social unrest and overt attacks by secular humanists were in full force against the Church of Jesus Christ. The church was being attacked externally from multiple angles by feminism, the sexual revolution, social reforms, widespread illicit drug use, normalization of divorce, and destruction of the traditional family, to name but a few. Internally, the attacks were more subtle and were a response to the external pressures. We were more interested in "sweet fellowship" with those harboring different sets of core beliefs (doctrine) than Scriptural accuracy. As a result, doctrine was sacrificed on the altar of a "feeling-oriented" gospel. A desire to feel good about ourselves as the church superseded our points of doctrinal difference.[51]

At the same time, the church was fighting another internal battle due to influence from liberal theologians. A groundswell of condemnation for the inerrancy of Scripture rose to a fevered pitch. As a result, some compromised and accepted a so-called middle position of *limited inerrancy*. Others deserted completely by adhering to a position of *infallibility*. As inerrancy was one of the two main doctrines of traditional evangelicalism, what was once a word encompassing many had again become a word describing the few.[52] Many today still refer to themselves as evangelicals, yet as we trace the meaning of the word, we see clearly there are few evangelicals as the word was originally defined. Evangelical has become a loose word, tossed about by many, including the media, but truly understood and practiced by a small minority.[53]

As evangelicalism gave way to secularism, its theological boundaries expanded. This expansion erodes the practice of thinking biblically, in particular, as it pertains to the nature of man and behavior. Theology became an embarrassing encumbrance as believers turned inward upon self, replacing biblical knowledge and understanding with self-knowledge and understanding. Left with two faiths, one in God and the other in man's theories, theology is diluted and God marginalized. God becomes nearly irrelevant to the everyday problems and difficulties of life. The church's interest in the supernatural is supplanted with the natural. The proof is in our everyday language. Instead of saying God's Word says such and such, we talk about our feelings, moods, compulsions and disorders. Have we not substituted psychology for theology? How dare we talk about defending the inerrancy of Scripture,

---

51 David Tyler & Kurt Grady, *Deceptive Diagnosis: When Sin is Called Sickness*, (Bemidji, MN: Focus Publishing, 2006), p. 111.

52 Sproul RC. *Faith Alone: The Evangelical Doctrine of Justification*, Grand Rapids, MI, Baker Books, October 2002. Chapter 1.

53 *Ibid*. p. 111.

which is the front door of the Christian faith, while we smuggle the sufficiency of Scripture out the back door, via theological compromise with psychology.

Many Christians today have chosen the path of compromise. They have withdrawn their Christian viewpoint from the discussions of behavior, moods and feelings. When they enter these fields of discussion they are compelled to accept a secular frame of reference. They use the secularist's language of diseases, disorders and addictions. They are convinced a Christian vocabulary is not only inadequate, but seems foolish sounding when talking about the complexities of contemporary society. They remain silent, bringing no Christian judgment to bear upon the people's condition. They fear that if they preface their comment with "the Bible says" they will be accused of preaching. And so they have trained themselves or habituated themselves to think secularly. They have behaved, worshiped and prayed Christianly, but then go back to therapeutic thinking. This equates getting into counseling with getting out of theology.

In spite of the fact that evangelical churches have grown in numbers, size and ministries, there has nevertheless come a hollowing-out of conviction. The loss of the belief in the sufficiency of Scripture has led to an erosion of morals. While churches have grown larger in stature and in number, they have diminished in character and quality. Secularism's intrusion in the evangelical church has caused it to lose its moral bearings. The Divine is replaced by the human (ungodliness) and righteousness by the therapeutic (unrighteousness). The old quest for godliness is replaced by a quest for psychological wholeness. Psychological wholeness is the substitute for godliness and is therefore ungodliness. It inevitably leads to more unrighteousness, bad feelings and the search for self-understanding continues. Who are we now that we have lost our understanding of the nature of man? One psychology tells us one thing, another psychology tells us another. Do we surrender ourselves to a biological fate and admit we are just the sum of our genes?

The psychologizing of sin is the natural outcome of secularism. Sinners, who are naturally prone toward self-justification, despise the concept of sin. Sin only has meaning in a world where God lives. To declare God dead is, at the same time, a declaration that man is good. Psychology explains and justifies man's behavior by providing an overabundance of mental illnesses to which he has fallen victim. Therapeutic salvation—being made whole by therapy—has taken the place of justification by grace through faith in Jesus Christ.

Psychological explanations for sin are very appealing in an age of compromised beliefs and broken lives. The pastoral counseling movement of the late 1960s challenged pastors to address the problems believers experienced from a psychological standpoint rather than a theological and sinful standpoint. They reasoned that giving attention to the therapeutic view conveyed sensitivity and love and was non-judgmental. Church members were viewed less as sinners accountable to God for rebellious behavior and attitudes, and more like victims who had fallen into complex circumstances of life or emotional conditions over which they had no control. The pastoral counseling movement did not deny the sinfulness of humanity, but believed the sin approach would be counterproductive to helping people with problems. They recognized the way sin complicated the lives of many of their parishioners. However, they believed that to confront and condemn, however inappropriate, the behavior, would be better dealt with through acceptance, open and caring communication. The obvious implication is that the biblical approach, God's way, is inappropriate and would not be helpful.

To say that sin is not a popular topic in pastoral counseling today, in light of the realization of a more enlightened and psychologically aware clergy, would be an understatement. However, a new interest emerged among conservatives and evangelicals that redirected the focus from the psychodynamic processes back to the sufficiency of God's Word where it was for thousands of years.

The Nouthetic Counseling Movement[54]

The biblical counseling movement, like many other anti-psychiatry movements, arose in the 1960s. In 1970 Jay E. Adams, a Presbyterian minister and seminary professor, launched an anti-psychiatry movement among American conservative Protestants. Upon the publication of his book, *Competent to Counsel*, Adams, who staunchly believed sin was a central theme in counseling, was viewed as an extremist. However, Adams' thinking was stimulated by psychiatrists O. Hobart Mower, William Glasser, Thomas Szasz and others. These men, all psychiatrists, led an anti-psychiatry movement. Rejecting the whole notion of mental illness, Adams developed a system framed explicitly in theological terms and challenged the dominant conservative Protestant understanding which relied heavily on secular theories and therapies of man and his problems. Adams did not see people stricken by a mental disease that prevented them from acting autonomously, but enslaved to sin and needing freedom to act responsibly.

The conservative Protestant psychotherapists frequently referred to Adams as a "psychology basher." However, Adams

54 The word, "nouthetic" comes from the New Testament words nouthesis (noun) and noutheteo (verb). A nouthetic confrontation (one believer confronting another) consists of three basic elements. First, a nouthetic confrontation always implies a problem in the life of an individual. It presupposes the need for change. For example, David's adulterous relationship with Bathsheba required David's repentance and change. Second, the problems are solved nouthetically by a person-to-person verbal confrontation. The prophet Nathan confronted David verbally. The third element of a nouthetic confrontation is that it benefits the person and glorifies God.

For an in-depth analysis of the word, "nouthetic," read Jay Adams' book, *Competent to Counsel*.

often expressed high regard for psychology as a discipline that studied psychological, physiological and psycho-social topics. Adams' criticism of psychology was what he saw as psychology's interference with the theologian's and pastor's role of counseling. He strenuously objected to attempts to provide secular explanations and solutions, (whether psychological or psychotropic medications), to people who were experiencing non-organic problems of living.

Adam's vision, unlike other anti-psychiatry movements, was focused exclusively on the church, Christian schools and seminaries. Adams believed there was a legitimate use of psychiatry in the case of well-defined organic problems. Pertaining to psychiatric hospitals Adams believed they served a protective and disciplinary role for individuals whose behavior was so unacceptable as to threaten themselves or others.

Unlike those in the secular anti-psychiatry movement, Adams did not view man enslaved by a system of social control who needed to be liberated so he could live an autonomous life. Adams viewed man as being enslaved by sin who needed to be set free through the redeeming and sanctifying work of God. Sin, for Adams, was an all-inclusive and bona fide diagnostic category that would recapture behavioral problems that had been labeled diseases. He did not view problems as diseases or disorders to be diagnosed. Adams did not portray counseling as therapeutic treatment.

While evangelicals continued to embrace the psychologies, those who were more biblically-oriented were attracted to Adam's nouthetic counseling model.[ ] Pastors, whose counsel traditionally consisted of a prayer, Bible verse, and a reluctant referral, became excited about a comprehensive, practical model that was consistent with the Bible. The emergence of the idea that counseling is the work of the church in general, and the pastor and elders in particular, began to take hold. Pastors not

only preached, but they counseled. Adam's nouthetic model
has increased exponentially over the past several decades.

The Open Grave

Thomas Hardy's poem, *God's Funeral*, portrayed God, who
had died, as an invention of man. Man needed a Comforter and
so he created God. Hardy wrote in stanza eight,

And, tricked by our own early dream,
And need of solace, we grew self-deceived,
Our making soon our maker did we deem,
And what we had imagined we believed.

The funeral wake for God has been going on for centuries
as philosophers have whittled away at the absolutes of God's
existence and certainties of Christian doctrine. They say there
are so many unanswered questions, such as, "How can there be
a God or how can God be good when the world is filled with
so much hatred, war, disease and starving children?" They say
our ideas of God are formed from our earliest years, but are
modified as we grow and mature. The more complex life is, the
more we must transform God to meet our needs. Now science
meets our needs and so we carry God to His place of final rest.
We have murdered Him with our compromises as well as others
have with their outright denials.

Have we really killed God, God with a capital "G"? No, as
much as men would like to kill the Almighty, He is not dead. He
is alive and gives men the breath they use to talk of His demise.
He gives them the strength to carry out their mock burial. **"He
who sits in the heavens laughs"** (Psalm 2:4).

I submit that we need to lay aside all of our failed human
reasoning and return to the sufficient words of God in the Bible.
The Book so many continue to attempt to discredit or improve

upon is the only constant and tangible item in the church. It is not man-made, but God-breathed.

As we stand over the open grave, I pray you realize it is not Jehovah God who is dead. The foul and disgusting odor that is choking us is the same as that which has permeated the church for years. It is one of our man-made gods. It is the rotting corpse of the psychology-god we have been worshipping.

By all means, let us bury it.

God's Funeral

About the Author

David M. Tyler, a native of Illinois, has served as a pastor in Southern Baptist churches in Illinois and South Carolina. He holds a B.A. in Theology, an M.A. in Pastoral Ministry, and a Ph.D. in Biblical Counseling. Presently, Dr. Tyler is the Director of Gateway Biblical Counseling and Training Center, in Fairview Heights, Illinois (www.gatewaybiblicalcounseling.org). He is certified by the National Association of Nouthetic Counselors and the International Association of Biblical Counselors. Dr. Tyler is the Dean of the Biblical Counseling Department and Vice President of the Board of Directors of Master's International School of Divinity in Evansville, Indiana. He serves on the board of directors of Personal Freedom Outreach in St. Louis, Missouri. Dr. Tyler also lectures and leads workshops on biblical Counseling. He is the author of *Jesus Christ: Self-Denial or Self-Esteem, Self-Esteem: Are We Really Better Than We Think?* and co-author of *Deceptive Diagnosis: When Sin is Called Sickness* and *ADHD: Deceptive Diagnosis* (www.deceptivediagnosis.org).

God's Funeral